Joy in the Workplace

Creating Zones of Inspiration, Trusting Relationships, and Profitable Work Environments

by

Chris Alexander

Also by Chris Alexander:
Creating Extraordinary Joy CDs
Joy in the Workplace CDs
Creating Extraordinary Joy VHS/DVD
Joy in the Workplace VHS/DVD
Synergizing Your Business Handbook
Creating Extraordinary Joy
Catch the Wind with Your Wings
Synergy Life Mastery Audio Album
Synergizing Your Business Audio Album
Success Is Fun Audio Album

Publisher: 1+1=3 Publishing
www.SynergyLifeMastery.com
First Edition
Library of Congress Cataloging in Publication Data
Alexander, Chris, 1948-
Joy in the Workplace: Creating Zones of Inspiration, Trusting Relationships, and Profitable Work Environments.
Includes biographical references and index.

Special Thanks to Contributors:
Michael Pattinson, Barratt American
Bob Evans, Fletcher Jones, Mercedes Benz
Diane Owens, ACS

Project Credits:
Cover Design: Bonnie Toth, Creative Vision
Developmental Editor: Lori Covington
Copy Editor: Sharon Young

Contents

Introduction

You may have picked up this book feeling intrigued or even irritated about a title like *Joy in the Workplace*, and who can blame you for feeling cynical about such an unlikely combination of words? But I'm going to ask you to suspend your disbelief because I have seen joy in the workplace and know it exists and that it's practical, achievable, and highly profitable. All over the world, businesses, schools, and other organizations are tuning in to joy, using it to reduce staff turnover and to increase productivity, customer satisfaction, and profits.

I have always been fascinated with human behavior, and for the last twenty-five years my research has been about the potential of human performance in the workplace. As an Organizational Behavior Specialist, I have consulted and worked for corporations where dysfunctional communication and conflict cause low morale, lousy productivity, and negative adversarial relationships (nice words for "I hate my job"). The heart of the problem is frequently defensive fear stemming from a bad habit of treating others with disrespect. I coach senior executives and business teams on how to let go of fear, and how to communicate in more constructive ways. As communication and collaboration improves and fear subsides, employee relationships become more Synergistic, strengthening every facet of the business. It's as if . . . there's magic in the air.

People are motivated to excellence by a sense of belonging, personal recognition, money, meaningful work, personal growth, and achievement. For people to be motivated by desire — which is the key to extraordinary performance — they need a fear-free environment that delivers more than just a paycheck. The motivation and excitement to perform at an exceptional level comes directly from the joy experienced through intra- and interpersonal connections (Synergistic relationships). Synergistic workplaces foster a sense of emotional security, creativity, and synchronicity. People want to have fun and feel fulfilled while creating something greater than themselves, and Synergistic leaders can achieve outrageous goals by harnessing and directing the human desire to engage cooperatively in compelling, satisfying work. Wise business strategists have always understood the competitive advantage of a happy workplace.

One of the greatest sources of power in a business is the committed hearts and minds of the people – the unified creativity and energy of people who are excited about their work. Harnessing that commitment builds unshakable, unstoppable zones of inspiration and secure, highly profitable work environments.

In this book, I've tried to include a good mix of inspirational examples and step-by-step directions for creating joy in the workplace. Like most changes, achieving joy through Synergy means giving up old ideas, unhealthy ways, and opening up and trying some new techniques and strategies that may frighten you. In this book, you will learn about managers and employees who have gained greater personal and customer satisfaction and discovered how much fun it can be to get up and go to work everyday. If you're not enjoying work as you should; if you'd like to feel energized rather than drained; if, instead of getting stuck in the mire of distrust and competitiveness, you'd like to feel comfortable with and "affectionate" toward your colleagues, this book was written with you in mind.

Learning from the Masters

I've had the honor of learning many of the practical aspects of my profession from truly great masters of business. I've been given the trust and respect to implement my Synergistic solutions to many of the

toughest age-old motivational problems.

Once commitment and enthusiasm for Synergy are seen in the actions and activities of the CEO and senior executive team, a trusting environment takes hold and extraordinary achievements are possible.

People love to support an organization that exudes enthusiasm and creativity. It's fun and it's joyful. Sadly, these types of organizations are in the minority. On many occasions, I have been invited to visit companies where, on an individual work level, there is an emptiness, a lack of spiritual psychological and emotional satisfaction, stemming from hostile environments and long, demanding hours. Many of these organizations have more internal competition between senior executives, managers, and fellow workers than with market competitors – and the problem is increasing exponentially.

You are probably saying: "Well, business is a serious activity. It's all about paychecks, profits, and show-me-the-money-shareholders." I want to draw a clear distinction here. It is more about how you believe business should be conducted. If you are of the old school, you believe in hierarchy. I have found that hierarchy is a distancing philosophy that operates under an uneducated misconception that fear, intrigue, and manipulation result in success. What I learned from the masters was that successful business leadership is all about sharing information, relationship-building, and trust.

If you like people, you won't have a problem with

the idea of creating joy in the workplace and building relationship bridges. If you don't like people, or you're afraid of them, you're not going to like this very much.

For years I have known that great business masters and leaders were not the hyped-up image that the media portrays. My experience has shown that the brash, swash-buckling, all-about-me big personalities would fail time after time. Often in the past, I would cogitate over making such a personal judgement in a variable professional situation . . . and then . . . I received an advance copy of Jim Collins' *Good to Great* book – now a bestseller – and as I read his description on Level 5 leaders, my personal judgement was suddenly validated by empirical research. What a great day that was!

"We were surprised, shocked really, to discover the type of leadership required for turning a good company into a great one. Compared to high-profile leaders with big personalities who make headlines and become celebrities, the good-to-great leaders seem to have come from Mars. Self-effacing, quiet, reserved, even shy – these leaders are a paradoxical blend of personal humility and professional will. They are more like Lincoln and Socrates than Patton or Caesar." (Jim Collins, *Good to Great*, 2001)

In all the successful companies I have worked with, leadership is encouraged at all levels of the organization, and empowerment is seen as a strategic advan-

tage. A workplace leader is a committed, motivated individual who contributes energy, creativity, skills, and knowledge toward a common goal. This means that selecting the right people becomes a strategic key to success. By selecting the right people, you reduce conflict, motivational issues, and the need for hierarchal management. When individuals are empowered, self-directed, and motivated, rules and regulations are less important.

Why I Wrote This Book

When people ask me what this book is about, I try to answer in the clearest way possible: This book is about attraction and love; it helps people fall in love with their lives by helping them find joy in the workplace. To many people, it is difficult to reconcile the fact that a person may be a successful business consultant, a romantic, and perhaps even a philosopher. If my listener seems interested enough, then my fullest answer is that this book contains what I believe are the essential concepts for radically changing the world of work and the world of business by changing the way we relate to each other in the workplace. At an individual level, it's about expressing your passion for a particular way of working and finding the right place to do it and the right people with whom to do it. At a leadership level, it's about freeing people to be more creative and, consequently, more productive. At an ethical level, it's about doing things right.

The people who read this book may do so for any number of reasons, although the main reason I would expect is because they want to improve their work lives and are hoping for answers to the troubles that plague them at work. It doesn't really matter who you are – this book should prove useful to you. You can apply many of these suggestions to your entire life.

The World of Work is Changing

This book will be published at the same time of my PBS special of the same name. It is exciting to think that I'll be reaching an even wider audience; that a teenager working in a fast food outlet can be exposed to the possibility of creating joy in the workplace. I like the idea that grandfathers, small business owners, and college students will find more purpose and meaning in their daily activities. The workplace is changing once again, but this time we are reacting in a deeper, more spiritual way. The new millennium brings with it a deep dissatisfaction and a yearning for collaboration and connection. We are reaching beyond the idea of materialism and connecting with what we know really works. We are all looking for meaning and joy in our lives. And we are looking for it in the workplace.

I remember the old benevolent dictators of the past who took care of their employees, providing them with outstanding working conditions, nurses on staff to take care of that common cold, and nurseries for the children of mothers working on the production line. Yes, they were dictators but they were also warm, generous, and caring individuals who had built their businesses based on the American dream. In small towns all over the United States, you would find these great business leaders whose style of leadership was relative to the times. While this earlier society was more conformist and hierarchal, I can't help but think that if those leaders were running businesses today, they would have adjusted their style to be more Synergistic, while not losing their humanity and understanding that a business is only as good as the people in it. Then along came the corporate raiders during the '80s with their "greed is good" mantra – buying up the wonderful family businesses, breaking them down, selling them off, making oodles and oodles of money, and ultimately destroying a concept that took many decades to build.

So, the question now becomes how do we create joy? Not just for a moment of fleeting happiness or for a day of pleasure, but in our families, our sporting activities and hobbies, and in the context of this book, the workplace. It is tough, because a lot of people have given their loyalty to a company and after many years of dedicated service, they've been told that their services are no longer required. Nice words for: You're fired! How does an individual who embraces ethical values believe it is possible to create joy in the work-place? One answer to that question is that, often in life, tragedy, pain, and suffering serve as wake-up calls, awakening the spirit of reconciliation within our true, authentic selves. We cry out for connection with our deeper selves and ask, "Who am I? "What do I stand for?" "What is life about?"

Catastrophe or a loss of a job may at first appear to be a crisis, but ultimately it will equal gain because we learn to make prudent, wise choices. If we choose to journey within, then the pursuit of happiness and joy becomes attainable. As Socrates said: "The unexamined life is not worth living."

The first thing we need to examine is what our perception of life is all about. Understanding how we perceive things will assist us in directing our lives toward joy.

"My best advise?
Fall in love with what
you do for a living."
- George Burns

Chapter One
The Joy Solution

When people start wanting to come to work, start enjoying the people they work with and the place where they spend most of their waking hours, the organization changes as an organism, growing richer and stronger with the strength of its people. It becomes a world without fear – a world of play and creativity, growing and developing, positive and oozing with every increasing potential.

Researchers who have worked with concepts like joy and happiness have found that people who are happy are healthier, recover quicker from illness or injury, work more productively, are more creative, and have greater self-esteem and emotional balance. People who are happy at work don't need to take "mental health" days from their sick leave. They don't sabotage equipment or shirk their duties, and they never shoot one another. *Joy in the Workplace* helps

organizations change by helping people change, which translates into employee satisfaction resulting in billions of dollars gained. The question is, when it comes to your organization, are they billions gained or billions lost?

How do we bring joy into the workplace? The answer is in a single word with an expanded meaning . . . Synergy. Synergy is any process by which the total of something (say, efficiency) is greater than the sum of its parts. A physical example of Synergy is bread. You take yeast, flour, and water, none of which can be eaten alone, and you combine them with heat, ending up with a loaf of bread. More simply put, the chemistry that turns four basically inedible ingredients into the staff of life is a perfect example of Synergy!

Synergy at work is what happens when people join together to accomplish a goal. Sometimes the spontaneity that sets the condition for Synergy comes about because the situation is unique, such as when there is a disaster and everyone pitches in without question to clean up and bring about normality. Synergy may also occur when things get hectic and people have the chance to do work they don't usually get to do.

I have a colleague who once worked for the sales department of the Vermont Teddy Bear Company in Shelburne, Vermont. At Christmastime, this company really shifts into high gear and people rotate positions as necessary. One day, word came up from the factory floor that there was a great need to get the teddy bears ready for shipping. Several people went down to the factory where they brushed and dressed and boxed teddy bears for several hours, working as a team, helping each other get each bear presentable and ready to ship. They played music and lugged heavy boxes from one part of the floor to another. They had a ball! Years later, my colleague still talks about her time at Vermont as one of her most enjoyable work experiences. The fun of doing something new as a team made work fun, and having fun made the work more easily achievable: They caught up in no time.

Synergy is more than a physical interaction between components: It is a highly effective way of getting people to work together. Aside from increasing work efficiency, Synergy feels good: people *want* to work together. Companies that focus on Synergy succeed financially and interpersonally, with low turnover and little absenteeism. Synergy will increase employee and customer satisfaction. It will significantly decrease absenteeism and attrition as it decreases less-measurable problems like individual stress, bullying, scapegoating, and blaming. Synergy will let you keep your best employees longer, maximizing your training dollars. Synergy is not only an interesting scientific phenomenon: It could be the best business tool you will ever use.

Recently, the International Labor Organization found that Americans are working harder and longer

than anyone in the industrialized world. Japan used to out-work us, but we surged ahead over the last decade, working on average 137 hours (3.5 weeks) more per year than workers in Japan. We work about 6.5 weeks more than the British and approximately 12.5 weeks a year more than German workers. While governments such as France and Canada recognize a work week consisting of 35 hours, the U.S. has been laying people off while piling overtime hours on remaining workers. Whereas people in European countries typically have vacations of four to six weeks, Americans are lucky to get two.

The interesting thing is that, with all that extra work, we don't hear anything about Americans being happier and more fulfilled at work. It seems we are working extremely hard for no particular reason except for the fact that people tend to feel guilty if they are not producing at an above-average level.

> **"Success is being truly happy at**
> **what you do."**
> **- Tommy Lasorda**

I enjoy my work because it's fun, and I derive a great sense of purpose from seeing companies grow while their employees become more trusting, satis-fied, and joyful in their daily responsibilities. One of the most important aspects of making work more joyful is understanding the concept of directing and conserving energy. It's all about working smart rather than working harder. I don't have anything against hard work, but if it doesn't pay off in satisfaction, it leads to increased stress, domestic and child abuse, alcoholism, drug addiction, and violence. Bullying is becoming a well-known workplace problem as people with fragile egos, insecurity issues, and too much power take out their frustrations on those who work for them. People who are being bullied suffer like victims of other types of abuse – with decreased immune response, increased illness, and even chronic disease. We don't hear much about bullying (like other forms of abuse, it tends to be kept secret), but you will see more and more discussion about it on the Internet and in employment reform because it can lead to the kinds of violence that make the news.

Like murder, for example. According to the Bureau of Labor Statistics, in 1999 there were over 23,000 reported acts of non-fatal workplace violence in this country. In the year 2000, workplace violence (including assaults and suicides) accounted for 16% of fatalities in the workplace. Violence is always in the top three causes of workplace fatalities. I guess you could say work doesn't kill people, but that *people* kill people.

Between cutbacks, layoffs, and downsizing, the resulting increased workload on remaining workers, and the stress of wondering if you'll have a job at all next month, employees are suffering under increasing stress and a growing anger about the way the world of work is being run. Add that to recent economic conditions, and you have a powder keg in the making. Even if employees aren't actually murdering each other, character assassination and general mistrust between co-workers and labor and management are constants in many organizations. Widespread misery accounts for a well-known condition where the most likely time for a person to suffer a heart attack is on Monday morning – the start of the new workweek.

Obviously, heart attacks, physical and verbal assaults, and even petty disagreements that double the length of weekly meetings, cost companies money. Rapid turnover, absenteeism, and poor morale are the personnel equivalents of an ever-fueled fire, consuming profits while burning out people, too.

The opposite side of the coin is that it is possible to re-create the workplace, under a model that stresses humanity even as it builds profits. Even for those working in giant, multi-national corporations, the insights in this book can be used to transform your work section or your department. When the impact of these dynamic changes is felt, it tends to widen throughout the organization as others start to ask, "Why is that department doing so well? How can we improve ourselves?"

Laying a Foundation for Synergy

**"If you fail to prepare, you prepare
to fail."
- Unknown**

In the same way that you would lay a foundation to construct a building, laying a foundation for Synergy in your organization prepares you for success. Joy comes about when you have created the correct environment for Synergy to build and grow. Creating the environment entails cleaning up the organizational climate.

Challenging Personal Fear

Psychological fear has all the same feelings, symptoms, manifestations, and reactions as the fear one feels when threatened physically. The good news is that psychological fear can be set free, reestablishing the courage to be objective. Changing our outlook about fear will help us gain the strength to challenge the fear existing within us, which gets easier with each attempt.

Psychological fear is a coward and a bully. Like all cowards and bullies, once we take a stand and have the confidence to deal with fear, it leaves us. You will be amazed at how quickly your mind and body will respond. Struggling with or denying fear is the food it needs to exist.

I once heard a great Swami say, "Invite your fear to tea to discuss what it needs and satisfy it by giving it the attention it is demanding from you. Then invite it to leave."

"You have nothing to fear but fear itself."
- Franklin Roosevelt

If we don't recognize the fear, it can cause us to behave in ways that we do not understand. For example, if we have a fear of not being accepted or loved enough or we are afraid of success, we might choose to use all kinds of excuses and come up with many justifications for not continuing with an opportunity or relationship.

Choosing to become more aware of the fear we feel will consciously lead us to set fear free. We do this by challenging the fear and doing the very thing of which we are afraid.

If you are a shy person who is embarrassed to conduct business presentations, challenge yourself by joining Toastmasters International, or offer to be the emcee at your next business conference. If you have a fear of spreadsheets, computer software applications, or you are intimidated by a bully in the workplace, you can overcome all of these fears by preparing for each situation or experience. It's not about winning the war – it's about winning one battle at a time. You can and you will be able to change whatever you want by having the courage to make prudent choices.

Challenging Workplace Fear

The fear of being fired or demoted or the fear of being attacked personally or humiliated is a very real possibility in today's workplace. In many organizations, the fear of failing and the "blame game" are very prevalent. When a manager's behavior toward an individual becomes personally abusive and aggressive in an attempt to get the employee to conform to company policies or procedures, exactly the opposite happens. The employee, motivated by fear, will carry out the task but, internally, will experience resistance, resentment, and perhaps even thoughts of revenge. We need to recognize that fear decreases productivity, compromise, flexibility, and interpersonal communication effectiveness and can create emotional and mental illness.

The financial cost can be devastating and can normally be tracked back to poor management skills and personal insecurity.

The Causes of Fear in the Workplace

To eliminate fear in the workplace, you need to promote the growth and development of your people. Letting go and allowing people to make mistakes will build confidence and higher performance.

Recognize that everyone fails from time to time: the leader as well as those following the leader's vision.

Be tolerant by defining and expecting a learning curve. Expect humanness. Be trusting of those who have earned it, be honest and direct with those who have not, but not brutally so. The idea is to create zones of inspiration through education and personal growth.

"A sense of humor is part of the art of leadership, of getting along with people, of getting things done."
- Dwight D. Eisenhower

Building small, high-performance teams for maximum effectiveness and motivation will allow your people to feel a sense of belonging. Naturally, there are employees lazy and clever enough who attempt to get away with minimal efforts. It is this type of employee that will test your leadership ability. Human relations, vital as they are to employee motivation, must always be accompanied by a firm insistence on good attitudes and good work. The old joke that "firing will continue until motivation improves" is just that, a joke. Good leaders will turn conflict into Synergy.

Bad Policies

The fair and honest implementation of a bad policy can cause just as much damage as the unfair implementation of a good policy. Companies that strive for Synergy must be willing to revise policies that are outmoded, unfair, or useless. When policy gets in the way of smooth- running effectiveness and employee motivation, it is time to change.

Unbalanced Competitiveness

Unbalanced competition between employees results in a negative atmosphere and a hostile environment that undermine the goals of the organization. While people struggle over their personal need-to-win-at-all-costs endeavors, the results of their competitive actions create a space in which insecure leaders control. The best antidote to this kind of fearful workplace is a clearly-defined set of core values that creates a secure working environment encouraging people to work together to solve problems and rewarding everyone involved when a solution is reached. Companies that rely on "star players" are like football teams that only send out their quarterback: undermanned!

Unethical Communication

When an individual practices unethical communication, it stems from a win/lose mentality and a basis of insecurity and habitual thoughts of unworthiness.

Insecurity can play out in many different ways such as pretending to be confident and self-assured. Real confidence is an inner sense of well-being, where there is balance and harmony between mind, body, and spirit. Other ways that insecurity plays out range from, in the extreme, aggressive-defensive and stand-offish behavior, to apologizing and over-politeness.

In workplace relationships, unethical communication can bring about untold problems. The insecure person will tend to need inappropriate amounts of attention and will often take personal credit for team ideas and successes. Unethical communication is used to manipulate situations for personal gain and will create tension and rejection from fellow workers and customers.

"Fear, guilt, and anger are the great destroyers."

When it's all over, the unethical communicator will say, "See I told you so; I knew it wouldn't work." At times, insecure people try desperately to do something outlandish, just to be the center of attention. Maybe they'll act weird, be obnoxious, or choose extreme attention- getting strategies with unacceptable comments and aggressive behavior. Insecurity has to be validated from the outside to the inside, which leads to a dependency-type relationship. In relationships, in work, in friendships, in every walk of life, the insecure person becomes very needy.

Untrained Employees

Why should a business team be any different than a team of Olympic champions? Olympic champions train themselves and do whatever it takes to rise up and achieve the extraordinary. Their coaches continually work with them, and they are open to learning new skills. It is the responsibility of both the employee *and* the employer to enter into this world of continuous learning.

Distrust

Like fear, distrust paralyzes people, causing them to make bad decisions. Synergistic organizations should value honesty between the company decision-makers and every employee. Distrust causes a chain reaction, where if I do not trust you, I withhold information that you need in order to make good decisions. Consequently, you cannot make good decisions, which furthers my distrust of you. Also, once you realize that I'm withholding information you need to do your job well, you have every reason to distrust me.

Apathy

Apathy is a response to ongoing pain. In early psychological experiments, when animals learned that they would receive electric shocks no matter what part of the cage they were in, they laid down and gave up. Ongoing fear and distrust are root causes of apathy.

Hierarchism

"No man will make a great leader who wants to do it all himself, or to get all the credit for doing it."
- Andrew Carnegie

Relationship building and communication play a role in finding a sense of meaning in our daily work. Top down communication stifles creative problem solving and the desire to participate. Unfortunately, the motivational focus becomes a "have-to" rather than a "want-to." This means that a person will only do as much as they are told to receive their paycheck. And sadly, the hierarchal supervisor pays the person as little as possible to keep them. In companies all across America, this game is played without either party recognizing the individual value and mutual benefit of cooperation and teamwork. You can have a chain of command without having to worship it. Of relevance is opening up company business so that everyone on staff has the opportunity to suggest, make improvements, and participate in the real work of the organization.

The Story of Rupert, the Bank Clerk – Caught up in the "System"

Rupert awoke. He had slept heavily, a fitful night, tossing and turning – a night of racing thoughts and anxious images. Today is Rupert's first day at work.

For as long as he can remember, his father told him: "Son, you should get a secure job with a large company that will provide you with retirement benefits and health insurance."

He could still hear those words playing in his head the day he went for the interview at the bank; and when they offered him the job, he felt a sense of satisfaction knowing that his father would be proud of him. The next day, a sadness came over him at the thought of being cooped up in a cubicle all day long, dealing with numbers.

In his heart, Rupert was always a non-conformist and knew that this job would require a large degree of compromise on his part. His secret desire was to be a graphic artist, working on advertising design and animation.

When the alarm went off, he forced himself to get out of bed. Walking across the room to the window, he drew back the drapes. It was a cloudy day and it was as if it was connected to his grey body-on-droop-mood. "Why does it have to be like this?" he said, feeling the greyness of the clouds almost entering his body and weighing it down.

"I hate clouds. It's going to be a miserable day, I can tell." As he looked at himself in the mirror, he thought, "I wonder if I'll be acceptable. I'll just be quiet, the same as I was in school. That's what works. If you're quiet, nobody sees you."

As he fastens his belt, thoughts of school run through his mind: flashes of high school, primary school, his first day. "Oh, that was hell. I cried. I can still feel the pain. Everybody in a row, all standing, looking just like each other, those huge

women teachers."

"Rupert, this will be your desk; and, by the way, here at our bank, we prefer that it be kept tidy, just as you should be. Do you understand?"

"Yes, sir."

"Don't call me sir! My name is Ms. Ashworth."

"Yes, Ms. Ashworth."

"That's better. Now relax, Rupert. Later, you will be taken to the training school, where you will learn about the basics of our banking procedures. Let me make myself clear, Rupert. If you work hard, do what I tell you, be on time for work everyday, the bank is an excellent place for you to have a steady, long-term career."

"Yes, sir, I mean, Ms. Ashworth."

Rupert felt very uncomfortable. The environment seemed very formal. There was very little, if any, small talk. Being an outgoing, friendly, talkative person by nature, he tried to make eye contact with a few people that passed his cubicle. It seemed as if everyone was hurrying around with their shoulders hunched, heads down, virtually expressionless faces gazing right through him. He just sat there and waited and wondered if this was the right decision for him. Eventually, someone said: "Rupert, follow me . . ."

The day dragged on and although the information he received in training class was interesting, the monotony of the trainer's voice exhausted him.

"Well, how was your day, son?"

"Dad, I don't know if this is what I want . . ."

"Now, Rupert, when I was your age, I would have been thankful for an opportunity like this. You kids of today don't appreciate anything. It was different for me when I was your age. I would have to walk to work everyday, ten miles there, ten miles back, uphill both ways."

"Yes, Dad, but I didn't do anything today; I just sat there."

"They know you are there. Everybody has their own job

to do; the world doesn't revolve around you."

He'd heard his father say that so many times before, and the thought occurred to him that he would need to work on being more conformist and grown-up and not expect life to be fun anymore. After all, there were still another four days to the weekend or, as his dad put it, "Mondays to Fridays are unnecessary days, linking your real life, which only happens on the weekends." That night Rupert slept soundly, exhausted from the emotional impact of the day.

The next morning, as Rupert prepared for work, he realized that Ms. Ashworth reminded him of one of his elementary school teachers who seemed to delight in ridiculing him and a number of other classmates: "Rupert, only speak when you are spoken to! Didn't your family ever teach you that kids should be seen and not heard?" Embarrassed, Rupert would shut down completely. He realized that to assert himself meant trouble.

"Rupert . . ."

"Yes, Ms. Ashworth?"

"Were you on time for work today?"

"Yes, Ms. Ashworth."

"You will be in training again today. They're expecting you."

"Yes, Ms. Ashworth."

Ms. Ashworth, who was huge and dominant, was married to an outgoing, lively used car salesman, and she got the shock of her life when he left her for another man, which destroyed her ability to function in a feminine way, particularly around young men. She secretly harbored a hatred for these kind of men. She had developed a reputation for being a tough manager who got the job done. "I motivate by fear," was her motto. Most people, including the bank president, avoided Ms. Ashworth, but when they needed to talk with her, it would normally be in couched terms.

Rupert sat next to an odd looking young man with thick-rimmed glasses and a plastic pen pouch sticking out of his

shirt pocket. "What a geek!" Rupert thought. But he greeted him nonetheless, and they immediately struck up a friendship. After training school that day, Rupert and his new friend, Michael, went to the local bus station, arguing about their future careers at the bank.

Five years later, Rupert received his first good service award. Ms. Ashworth had now become the manager and Rupert the assistant manager. She seemed to have a glimmer of a smile as he walked up to her. "I told you you'd make it. Just do as you're told and one day you could be manager, too."

That night, as he and Michael talked, Rupert still felt an emptiness, a sense of dissatisfaction, and a lack of fulfillment.

"Rupert, I'm reading this book about finding your purpose in life. Once you do, you automatically become motivated and fulfilled. You must read it!"

"Oh, please, Michael! Motivation? What good will that do me at the bank?"

"Well, it says that everything in your life can change when you look at things differently."

"What do you mean?"

"That your success is tied up with your perception of life, your purpose, and how much passion you have for the things you do."

"Tell that to Ms. Ashole."

"I suppose you're right."

"Of course I'm right. My dad always told me: 'Do as little as possible and get as much as you can. Mondays to Fridays are unnecessary days, linking your real life, which only happens on the weekends.' I tell you, Michael, with a little luck, and a lot of brown nosing, we'll be promoted, and then it will be our turn to be the kings."

"It is the supreme art of
the teacher to awaken joy
in creative expression and
knowledge."
- Albert Einstein

"Work joyfully and
peacefully, knowing that
right thoughts and right
efforts will inevitably
bring about right results."
- James Allen

Chapter Two
Perception, Purpose, and Passion

Perception

Perception colors everything in our lives. We live with rainbows of possibilities or clouds of despair. How we perceive our world makes all the difference, because it determines much of our willingness to be motivated.

Ron's Story

Ron is a successful business owner in Southern California. He owns a "getaway" cottage in Big Bear Mountain. He is a car enthusiast and owns a number of late model sports cars. Often, he and his wife drive up to Big Bear to spend the weekend in a more relaxed environment. It was on one of

these occasions that he experienced the negative effects of seeing something one way when in reality it was the opposite.

Half way up the mountain, as he looked ahead up the road, he saw a car careening down the hill. His body flooded with adrenaline as he sensed the danger of the oncoming car as it swayed from one side of the road to the other. His mind raced . . . should he stay where he was or should he move to the other side of the road to avoid a collision? He decided to hold steady and slow down, while staying on his side of the road. He is fixated on every move of the oncoming car and as it gets close, it swings back onto the correct side of the road. As it skims past him, a woman sticks her head out the window and screams, "PIG!" To which he thinks, *what*! How dare she call me that! Pig? Me, a pig? And without hesitation he retaliates at the top of his voice, "SOW!" . . . and as he turns the corner he slams into the pig . . .

We need to look at our perceptions and the way we relate to the new workplace because it is a completely new workplace that requires new ways of thinking. Today you can work for an organization for thirty years and come in one day and learn that the company has been sold or that the corporate office has decided to downsize, and your services are no longer required. That's the way it is and in this new workplace, we need to reduce our dependency and become more entrepreneurial.

When you come to work with an entrepreneurial spirit, you come to work with a different mind set that you're actually doing a project for your company. You get more involved because the only security you have, really, is that of doing a great job.

Entitlement no longer exists. Your job is only as safe as the emotions of the person who hires and fires you. In today's workplace, you're going to find as much bizarre behavior in a prestigious law firm as you will in an all-night video store, and as much altruism and compassion in a restaurant as in a medical clinic. Jobs aren't just jobs – they are places where people gather to act out stories, to form relationships, and to impact each other. The places we work are more than just desks and computers and gas pumps and mail rooms. They are compendia of human behavior, running the gamut from healthy and delightful to freakish and sad.

**"Life is a great, big canvas and
you should throw all the paint
on it you can."
- Danny Kaye**

The Dalai Lama said this about Westerners' focus on their careers: "...when I talk to people of various professional backgrounds, particularly from the West, they seem to have a tremendous amount of attachment to their profession... people seem to have an enormous personal investment in their profession, they identify with it, so much so that they feel as if their profession is so vital for the world's well-being that if it were to degenerate the whole world would suffer. This seems to me that their level of

attachment is inappropriate." (*Transforming the Mind*).

He's right, of course. We are hung up on our jobs, and what they mean about who we are. When we're little, we instinctively understand that work is part of life, and we make it part of our play. We choose the occupations that look glamorous and fun to us and decide to be firemen and ballet dancers and actors and brain surgeons. The world of work seems a lot more interesting when you're five! It's only later that other considerations come in and we get hung up on things like where we are on the corporate ladder, how much money we [don't] make, and whether it's too late to become a brain surgeon. In one way, it's vital that you work at something that excites and challenges you. In another way, what you do doesn't matter if you're hampered by a dysfunctional workplace because it's difficult to get *anything* done when you're just trying to avoid being stabbed in the back!

The fact is, whether you're starting a career as a physical therapist or working a job in a retail store, you will encounter the same sorts of behaviors from others, experience the effects of company culture on your thoughts and well-being and from time to time, feel the ennui that marks the fact that you aren't hanging out, aren't enjoying yourself, but that you are, in reality, working. The status or seeming permanence of your current position is irrelevant: Working is a complex process that involves every part of your person, every part of your life, whether you intend it to or not. Bad work can make you physically and mentally ill: It can diminish you spiritually and morally. Good work, joyful work brings out your best attributes, puts you in fine-tuned and harmonious relations with others, and lets you be fully human, fully present and engaged. The difference between good work and bad work is not so much the actual "doing" of the job, although this does play a role, but your intention and the intentions of those who lead in that particular workplace. Are people valued or discounted, trusted or maligned? Are they perceived (and treated) as costs to the organization or as the precious assets they truly are?

When we talk about the world of work, what does it mean to you? Does it make you smile, do you cringe inside? Is work a painful necessity and the thing you do between the weekends, or is it the thing you do because it brings you joy?

For most people, work is not the happy part of life. For many, it is uncomfortably close to torture. You're not imagining things: The world of work can be a dangerous place, but it really doesn't have to be that way.

The major purpose of this book is to explain the ways that work can become a work of art, poetry in motion, meaningful and life-affirming. Work, depending on your perception, can be the purest expression of your soul.

"Joy comes from using your potential."
- Will Schultz

Crisis=Opportunity

We are in the middle of a crisis. Work has taken on a life of its own and seems to be making demands on our lives and families, and most people are having difficulty coping with the increased pressure. Here's the good news: Crisis is good! People don't know it yet, but within these demands lie the seeds of freedom and joy.

The reason I say that crisis is "good" is because crisis demands change, and change, although terrifying, is the quickest way to increased opportunity. The word "crisis" makes me angry because it seems that the people who are describing the latest crisis often have a motivation for wanting me to view it negatively and panic. When we hear about unemployment crises, we hear it from the media who are highly invested in brokering fear. Fear sells magazines. Crises sell fear. Selling fear is all about fostering certain perceptions in the general public. As members of the general public, you and I can decide how much to attend to, how much to believe. We can choose our perceptions.

I'm not nearly as worried about the *un*employment crisis as I am the *employment* crisis. If everyone who's unhappy at work decided not to go tomorrow, the country would come to a grinding halt. I think it's critical that so many people are so unfulfilled at work. There are a number of simple solutions to the misery we see in today's workplace. And with a little attention, and the return to ethical ideas like kindness, honesty, and leadership, we can change the workplace into zones of inspiration where trusting relationships and profitable work environments can be of benefit to both internal and external customers. I have seen large, profitable corporations embracing the power of relationships to achieve high performance. They are the breeding grounds for productivity and employee satisfaction.

"There is joy in work. There is no happiness except in the realization that we have accomplished something."
- Henry Ford

At Southwest Airlines, for example, relationships, mutual respect, and communication excellence are of paramount importance in creating a sense of meaning and joy in the workplace. In my opinion, one of the keys to Southwest's success is understanding that people want to work in an environment that is enjoyable, and customers want to deal with a company that exudes enthusiasm.

The majority of people within the organization — including the leadership (starting with Herb Kelleher, Chairman of the Board; James Parker, CEO; and

Colleen Barrett, President and COO) – believe that Southwest Airlines was created by its people.

Words like fun, celebration, compassion and innovation shore up the company values which are held in high esteem. The most profitable airline in the U.S., Southwest not only maintains a spirit of "fun" but has also had the ability to "synergize" a number of different areas; thus, its well-orchestrated strategic coordination has created a competitive advantage that is difficult to match, a testimony to that old adage: When teamwork, quality, and service go up, costs come down.

Laughing and having fun with the customer is an important part of Southwest's focus. As such, humor is encouraged at every level of the organization, from the inside out, with people thinking humorously, smiling, laughing, and making work, play. At Southwest, people are hired for their attitudes and *then* trained to develop their skills. Simply put: Southwest Airlines is comprised of the most productive workforce in the airline industry.

> **"Never doubt that a group of
> thoughtful committed citizens
> can change the world, indeed it's
> the only thing that ever does."
> - Our Values, The Body Shop**

"If it's not fun, why do it" is one of the phrases you will hear at Ben & Jerry's. According to Ben Cohen and Jerry Greenfield, "Everything we do in our business is value-led" and it's true that their success has been based, in large part, on their connection with human values.

From the very beginning, one of their sayings was: "How can we serve you better?" It wasn't just a customer service training line, it was for real and they meant it. That sincerity and steadfastness has earned a kind of customer loyalty that most corporations pay millions to achieve. Ben & Jerry's works from the age-old principle: "As you sow, so shall you reap" or in the terminology of this book, they focused on Synergy – seeking out ways to serve so that the sum was always greater than the separate parts.

In 1978, Ben & Jerry's started out with three goals:
1) To have fun
2) Make a living
3) Give back to the community

As the company grew, they connected with many others who felt the same and their ideals began to become reality. In Ben & Jerry's words: "Value-led business is based on the idea that business has a responsibility to the people and the society that make its existence possible. In order to do that, values must be led and be right up there in a company's mission statement, strategy, and operating plan. This gives the employees and customers a relationship that is based on more than money.

> **"I couldn't ask for a better company . . .**
> **when you have been treated so well,**
> **it's hard not to appreciate it. And I'm**
> **not the only one – that's the best part**
> **of it. They do it for everyone."**
> **- Julie Labor, Production Line Worker**

It's okay to have fun, and it's okay to be joyful. Ben & Jerry's has created what they call "The Joy Gang" with this mission: "To keep work from being a grind." The Joy Gang plans fun events ranging from bi-monthly massages for workers to an Elvis-Presley-day, that includes an Elvis impersonator and look-alike competition, the whole idea being to bring joy into the workplace. To top that, the company has an outstanding benefits package! Now that's caring capitalism at its best!

Recently, Ben & Jerry's was sold to Unilever, and it will be a great day for business if their social mission slowly influences the worldwide conglomerate.

Reality and Change

I have been in the same room with people who love their work, who look forward to its challenges, its twists and turns. And most of these people are not wealthy or CEOs. I have met a number of millionaires who were downright miserable because, like the Beatles song, "Money Can't Buy Me Love." Loving relationships are the finest and sweetest part of life. Good relationships on-the-job will make work, any kind of work, meaningful, profitable, and joyful. And maybe the hardest part of turning work into a web of excellent relationships is in believing that it's possible.

Perceptions about work start in childhood. Remember when Dad came home and sank into a chair, took off his shiny shoes, flexed his sweaty feet, and grouched at you not to bother him? He read the paper, watched a ball game, and maybe even demanded absolute silence. He had a "hard day" at work and coming home was his chance to "relax." Are these the behaviors of someone who had an invigorating, exciting, enjoyable day at work? Maybe you saw this when you were little and thought, "Oh boy, work surely must be some awful place. Hope *I* never have to go there!"

Now, contrast this with Mr. Rogers, the children's public television star. He would come through the door, hang his suit jacket neatly in the closet, pull out a powder-blue cardigan, remove his shiny shoes, and put on his play shoes. Then he would take us into wonderland. Mr. Rogers was coming to work, a gentle, loving, imaginative place where people were friends, where disagreements were solved, where he was happy.

What if everyone's work felt like Mr. Rogers' neighborhood instead of a battle zone? It can! Why should you believe that assertion? You don't have to yet: Just keep an open mind. Remember when your

work was to copy the alphabet on that big, lined paper with a fat pencil? Or to draw a picture with as many colors as you wanted? Or to dance to the music from the recordplayer? Remember how much fun it was to try hard, and to succeed? The work has changed, but your possibilities haven't. Allowing the possibility that work can be a happy place is the first step in recreating work as a joyful place.

That Old American Dream

Our other perceptions, or frames of reference, might not be so much impressions we received in childhood as expectations our parents foisted upon us. A lot of parents tell their kids, "Go to school, get a good education, get into a good college, get a real job with a good corporation that has health care and a good retirement package. Then you can retire and do all the things you 'really' enjoy for the rest of your life." As if work is this awful place that must be endured until you reach the joyful part of your life.

That is a powerful story, and it's amazing that in the face of decades of the most pernicious downsizing, it persists. This perception, which is a part of the American Dream, says that if you do your best (notice that doing your best doesn't include *enjoying* your long-term job), you will be rewarded by the father-figure corporation, which will meet all your needs, all your life. It may seem wrong to dismantle a part of the "dream" but letting go of this perception will open the possibility to a true pursuit of happiness. If you happen to be a person who has found a haven that expresses this story, that's great, but if you are expecting this story to be the norm in your work life, you will most likely be disappointed.

All over our nation parents are dismayed and saddened when their skeptical teenagers point out that there is no such thing as job security, and question that a college degree is worth the time and effort. We need to refocus our efforts on educating ourselves and our children that true joy is possible by moving away from the father-figure expectations to finding a personal sense of purpose. Public education started in this country as a way of providing the necessary workers to the newly industrialized workforce. Factories needed people who could tell time so they would show up promptly to work, and they needed people who could both read and write a little. The idea that children should attend school arose from the need for slightly more educated workers. Unfortunately, the American Dream (to get a good job) usurped in our consciousness the other reason for getting an education, which was to lead a more learned and informed life and ultimately to be of greater service to others. So now, when a kid says, "Why should I get an education when it no longer guarantees me a decent job?", parents stand there with their mouths open, trying to think of something to say. Maybe they say, "Because I said so, that's why!", which may get some initial results but can hardly be called a logically compelling argument.

> **"Real joy comes not from ease or
> riches or from the praise of men, but
> from doing something worthwhile."**
> **- Pierre Coneille**

We're caught between the old story of what work should be and by what it has actually become. And the incongruence between what we want to believe and what we experience is so great that it leads us to grab up new expectations, to armor ourselves against the unknown. Suddenly told to expect nothing, we reach for anything. Frankly, people get some weird ideas about what they are entitled to in the workplace. They feel cheated when the espresso runs out and become incensed over parking space issues. Some people actually believe that they are entitled to special favors from others in their workplaces – they see this as a power perk! The issue of entitlement is a reflection of the insecurity inherent in today's workplace – a human reaction to chaotic conditions. It's not really because people are insane, it's more of the soul's expression of confusion about what we are really getting out of going to work.

Bizarre Perceptions: Misplaced Entitlement

I knew a university department where the union for the staff members was quite strong. One secretary was famed throughout the college for not working under any circumstances. She brought a small television to work and watched soap operas while sitting at her desk. When people tried to get her to work, she made such a mess that they never asked again – I never saw her do a thing, so I can't say for sure. Her expression, which was mostly hostile, was enough to protect her from the evils of the copier, the computer, and the filing cabinet. And because no one was going to take on the union, she sat there, year after year, occupying a workspace, denying a productive, enthusiastic person the opportunity of self-fulfillment.

> **"The world is full of willing people.**
> **Some willing to work, the rest**
> **willing to let them."**
> **- Robert Frost**

Can you imagine the perceptions she must have had about her work? Can you imagine working at the same level in an organization with someone whose main personal goal is to be vastly unproductive? Can you imagine supervising such a person? The sheer exhaustion of it boggles the mind. She felt entitled to do nothing – maybe because she'd been at that desk for fifteen years. Or maybe because she had internalized the idea that you're "entitled" to anything you can get away with. And while her story might be, "I'm taking what I'm entitled to," the effect was that she had no opportunity

to participate in the fun of work. One other secretary, who was a junior version of herself, ate lunch and talked on the phone with her. The other secretaries avoided her, as did the faculty members and students. In effect, she was the departmental pariah. Imagine going home at the end of every day knowing you hadn't done a single thing and that apparently no one cared or needed, or even missed you.

Khalil Gibran said that if you can't love your work, you may as well take up a begging bowl. He wasn't being sarcastic. In Buddhism, there is an idea that the beggar has a natural place in the social order. The beggar gives the rest of us the opportunity to be generous, which enlarges our spiritual well-being. The beggar is doing us a favor, braving the elements, hunger, and the stingy in order to reach those who are ready to give. The beggar, in this light, according to this perception, is the generous one.

Perceptions can be devastating to your reality. Let's say you go to a party, and right before you get there, someone tells you that the hostess said something particularly nasty about you last week. But you have to go to the party because you're supposed to network with someone you have few other chances of seeing. So you go, but you're miserable the whole time. Your hostess greets you at the door with a warm hug and you think, "You hypocrite, get your hands off me," but you don't say anything. You're angry — what did you ever do to her? Boy, would you like to tell her off! Or, feeling hurt, you really wish you could ask her what you did to make her hate you so much. The whole party is colored by your unhappiness. But once you get home, you check your messages and find out that it was a complete misunderstanding. Your informant feels terrible – he had simply heard wrong.

Suddenly, you see the party in a different light. Your perceptions have changed.

If you aren't already happy at work, take time to think about your perceptions and expectations. Some are realistic, but some may be open to interpretation. Which ones can you afford to throw away? Which ones can be replaced with more optimistic ideas? Notice what your co-workers' perceptions are, too. Look around you – who's happier? Who's chronically grouchy? Who's celebrating? Who's always sick?

> **"Seven days without laughter**
> **makes one weak."**
> **- Mort Walker**

I don't have a lot of naive ideas about the workplace. I have seen too many organizations where sickness, psychological warfare, and plain old mean-spiritedness are intrinsic to the culture to make up stories about how cut-throat, corporate America is a "natural" outgrowth of capitalism. They may not actually murder you with spears, but they might smear you with honey and tie you to an ants' nest.

It's all a matter of degree. So I'm certainly not advocating a blind, trusting smile without any discrimination between friend and foe in your workplace. I'm just saying that, if the place you work isn't inherently dangerous to your well-being, there is a chance that you can dump some old baggage and be happy there. If you're in a place that you recognize as chronically unhealthy and unlikely to change, the best thing you can do for yourself is look for something better.

Purpose

**"Man is a stubborn seeker
of meaning."
- John Gardner**

Why do you go to work? If you're like most people, your answer is, "I work for the money." To some extent, everyone works for money. But some people work for scads of money in order to buy expensive cars, houses, or clothes. Some people work for nearly nothing, supporting another passion that has yet to pay off financially. The artist in the garret is one example. Some people work so their children can have a better life. Too many people struggle, working to pay for mortgages so they'll have a place to live that's near work. There is a commercial that makes me sad every time I see it. It's a short story about a young man who lives in a tiny apartment and works at a meaningless job. His one source of satisfaction is the drive to work in his new car. "We were made for better things – when did it become acceptable to sell your very self for a mid-priced automobile?"

While we're throwing out old baggage and challenging old perceptions, fear rears its ugly head again. The main reason many people go to work at all is because they're afraid of being fired. For some people, it's a legitimate fear – they have children to care for, a house to support and, in a turbulent economy, they may not have a lot of choices about where and how to work. But some people have gotten into the habit of this fear so that when new opportunities arise, they don't even see them.

"None are so blind as those who will not see."

It's scary to make a change, even a change for the better. When a logging area is all logged out or there's a moratorium on fishing (and although the government may institute training programs for employees), many loggers and fishermen (or corporate trainers or HR people) do not take up the challenge to learn other ways of working. Logging and fishing are physically hard, highly dangerous jobs, but the fear of losing one particular way of life blinds us to other possibilities, even when the original job is no longer a practical option.

"There is no more fatal blunderer than he who consumes the greater part of his life getting his living."
- Henry David Thoreau

Fear motivation will keep some people in jobs that don't fit them properly, but they are constantly exhausted from the effort of doing something that doesn't feel right. Out of fear, kids entering college may decide to become accountants rather than artists, managers rather than musicians. What they don't see until later is that you can be as pragmatic about career choices as any career counselor, but in the end, the needs of your soul will vanquish all those practical intentions. One of the greatest gifts parents can give their children is the outspoken permission to do what they enjoy, all the way through school and right into a career. It may seem like a good solution to push kids into "practical" careers, but in the long run, it causes pain and confusion. Better to start out headed in the right direction than to start over after years of dissatisfaction.

Defining your real purpose in working may be the inspiration of a moment or an ongoing saga. Some people will know what they want from the start and will pursue it always. These are the lucky few. More people tend to have several careers over the course of a lifetime. Some folks just flounder, trying one thing, then another.

**"One of the symptoms of an approaching nervous breakdown is the belief that one's work is terribly important."
- Bertrand Russell**

Your purpose is the way you claim your destiny. If you know what you love to do, and do it, your life will be richer than if you settle for less. Choosing your life's work is arguably as important as choosing your mate – after all, most people can expect to work for decades. What's more frightening: making a big change that reflects your innermost desires, or the possibility of wishing all your life for something you could have had but were afraid to try?

Integrity of purpose is vital to being willing to provide important basics like excellent customer service. If you're excited about what you're doing, proud of your work, your products, happy about where your company is headed, you'll want to share those feelings with everyone you meet. On the other hand, if your workplace has nothing to do with what you care about, you're going to start to resent it. Resentment is a strange emotion, much more complicated than fear, anger, or even shame, maybe because it embodies elements of all three. Rather than resenting myself for choosing a career path that is unfulfilling to me, I will invariably start to resent my boss, the company, or my co-workers. Focusing my

resentment on externals gives me the illusion that someone else is responsible for my discontent. If I start wondering, "Why have I chosen this path?" it puts the responsibility for doing something back on me. And that's a lot of pressure, isn't it? On the other hand, recognizing that the ball's in my court also gives me options that I don't have if someone else is in charge of my life. So, if you aren't yet sure of your purpose but you know you don't like where you are, put aside the terrorist boss, the unfair company, and the lousy pay structure and ask yourself, "What do I really feel passionate about? What turns me on?" Think hard about what makes you happy, and then get to work!

External Blocks to Purpose

The main internal blocks to acknowledging and expressing your work's purpose are fear and procrastination. External blocks may include the lack of support of family and friends, a political, competitive, hierarchical workplace that wears you down, or a boss with the personal characteristics of a terrorist. Being driven crazy at work is a surefire way to make your purpose seem hopelessly irrelevant. You're just hoping to get through the next meeting without stapling someone's mouth shut. If your workplace cannot support the growth and expression of your purpose, it's time to start looking for someplace that can.

If you're pretty clear on your purpose, take a look

at your current workplace and appraise it in terms of how much you can realize your purpose there. If in general you're in the right place, it may just take a little tweaking to align your job with your purpose. If you're working in a fast food place and your purpose is to be a graphic artist, it's time to get to the drawing board and redesign your life. Are you taking classes in graphic arts and multimedia design? What's the first step? Take it, and then take another.

If expressing your purpose requires a change of corporate venue, make your job interviews work for you. You don't want to promise everything and get nothing – that would be a huge waste of your time. Most interviews end with the prospective employer asking the employee if s/he has any questions. This is your primary chance to find out if this is the right place for expressing your purpose. Ask what the company culture is like: If the interviewer doesn't like the question, you're probably in a place where hierarchy matters. If you don't already have a clear picture, ask how the company is run. How long do people tend to stay at the company? What are current projects and plans for the future? What's the training situation like? If the interviewer can't answer one of your questions, you might think twice about the amount of information distributed at various levels of the organization.

You can pick up the general vibe of a place from the receptionist. Is s/he friendly? Open or uptight? Formal or casual?

Ask a few questions: What's the boss like? Are you involved in a regular training program? Have there been any layoffs lately? The answers you receive will reveal a lot about the culture of that company.

Making Authentic Choices

> **"If the mind is happy, not only the body but the whole world will be happy. So, one must find out how to become happy oneself. Wanting to reform the world without discovering one's true self is like trying to cover the whole world with leather to avoid the pain of walking on stones and thorns. It is much simpler to wear shoes."**
> **– Ramana Maharshi**

Discovering and living out your purpose goes hand in hand with making authentic choices. The day you sigh and say, "Well, it looks like I'm really an actor/ chef/ mechanic/ runic scholar," is the day you've made the most important, authentic choice of your life: the announcement of your purpose. After that, it's a matter of making more of the right choices, the ones that fit your purpose most closely, over and over again. Making authentic choices isn't only about choosing the right place to work – it's about how you express yourself in general. The cliché about painters living in garrets makes sense because painters have to live somewhere cheap until they're established artists. Basements are usually the cheapest places, but painters can't paint in basements because they need light in order to realize their passion. So they take attics and the tops of old warehouses. They swelter in the summer and freeze in the winter, but they gain the advantage of that great, high-up light. It's part of being a painter.

When you know what you want, making authentic choices comes easier than when you're not committed to a course of action. Once you know your purpose, there will be all sorts of decisions to make, some of which will distract you from your purpose. Do you take the job that offers a basic salary but cuts into time you'd otherwise spend at the library researching your novel? Do you go into business with your brother because he needs a partner, even though you've never really been interested in window coverings? It's like a driver's education film where you've got a bicycle to the right and slightly in front of you, a tailgating bus just behind, and a pedestrian crossing the street just any damn where he feels like. Then a guy in a Pinto runs a red light and makes a left turn in front of you. It's hard to decide which mistake to make first!

What can you do when things are distracting you

from your true purpose?

First, slow down. Take some time to meditate on the changes you want to effect and changes that you might be tempted to make purely for the sake of changing. Sometimes, when you panic that things aren't working out as quickly or easily as you'd hoped, it's tempting to take any new job or apartment or lover, just to feel like you're in some control. If you find yourself making changes in a blind panic, take a break and remind yourself of what matters most to you.

Think Synergy. Synergy describes what's happening when the total is greater than the sum of its parts. When it comes to work, it means that if one person takes four, jaw-clenching hours to complete a task, two people may complete the task with laughing and jokes in an hour and a half. Four people can get the job done in about thirty-five minutes, and it'll be a party. A work group that has Synergy can accomplish more than larger groups or even more skilled groups where Synergy isn't part of the process. Synergy is when everything flows, creativity is rampant, people cooperate to create the best solutions, and everyone's having a great time.

For the individual pursuing her/his passion, Synergy at work is a natural part of the process. It's when you discover that three hours have passed in a flash while you worked on something that totally involves you. Like many wonderful phenomena, Synergy can't be forced – it just happens. Still, we can encourage the growth of Synergy in our work by being attentive to the needs of the self, and by not being overly influenced by other people's expectations. For example, if you are my publisher and expect these pages before noon each day, you may be disappointed to discover that before noon, I'm not much of a writer. I need to get into my day, clear my messages, solve some problems, and work my way gradually to the manuscript.

Encouraging Synergy in your work life requires a certain amount of self-understanding and enough flexibility in your workplace to meet your needs. If you need a quiet, serene atmosphere in which to design a new car seat, but you work in a cubicle in the middle of a raucous sales office, it's a waste of your time and energy to try to ignore your creative needs. Ideally, you have a boss and a schedule that lets you set the pace. Less than ideal is a micro-managing boss who doesn't believe that people will work without being closely attended. Micro-managers who mean well can usually be reasoned with. Horrific is the terrorist boss who probably knows you could do the work better in another situation but who takes pleasure in making work extra difficult for you. Terrorist bosses, who will not be reasoned with, deserve to be left alone with their weird enjoyments while you find someone better with whom to work. If your capacity for Synergy is being interfered with, it's up to you to find a way to change the situation.

Firing Your Boss

I am a consultant, so in a way I'm the master of my own destiny. In another way, anyone who pays my fee is, for a time, my employer. But I have walked away from projects when my employer didn't measure up. A large part of my job is to educate business leaders about ways to run their organizations with integrity, and most of the time that's a satisfying job. But once in awhile, I run into someone whose agenda wasn't ever to actually improve his organization. Sometimes people have hired me because other people wanted them to, or wanted to appease employees or convince themselves that they had done all they could (without actually doing much of anything). Once I stood in a room with a bunch of employees and listened to the CEO give a speech about all the wonderful things he was putting into place for his workers. They were happy! They applauded him. He was the Big Man on Campus. But within days, the Big Man laid off a large percentage of his work force. Seems the temptation for a little momentary stockholder gain was too much to resist. I felt used. I was disgusted at his duplicity, the way he'd let his company down, his lack of thought regarding the remaining employees and the effect of his actions on many areas of the business. Following his layoffs, a rash of resignations followed and not long afterwards, he was fired. I wonder what he will screw up next? One of my core values is that I have to be able to trust and respect the people with whom I work. So I took him to lunch at a famous restaurant in Orange County and fired him.

Sometimes you can do everything right, but if the people you work with are playing by a different set of rules, everyone is losing. Ideally, it should be possible to tell at an interview if you're headed into a bad place, but interviews are like first dates: It's difficult to really know what you're getting before you're already committed. If the people you work with aren't interested in playing by the rules you find important (especially in matters of integrity and honesty), the wise thing is to get out as soon as you realize that your values aren't shared by your co-workers.

> **"There are those who give with joy,**
> **and that joy is their reward."**
> **- Kahlil Gibran**

Passion

Bring your passion to work, and come to work on purpose. You have to love your work and feel it's worthwhile, or find something you can become passionate about and make it worthwhile. Obviously, no one's going to be delighted with every aspect of their work all the time, but it's vital to have a central core of enjoyment or pleasure so that when things get tough, you still have the emotional security to get you through. If you ever watch the Food Net-

work, you'll see people who are in love with their jobs. The chefs talk about the food, compare flavors and colors, taste and smell things, and have a great time doing it. But the next time you go to a restaurant, look at the chaos, the heat and flames in the kitchen, the demanding physical aspects of the work. To be a chef, to work all day and half the night on your feet in a hot kitchen with people yelling, dishes clattering, and hungry, cranky customers, well – you'd better love food!

When you love your work, it's easy to commit to being great at it, to seek out improvements in yourself, and to challenge yourself by taking on new tasks or learning new skills. When you are committed in this way, you are modeling passion and commitment to your employees. Your commitment to greatness also has impact when you direct your passion towards the most important people in the business – the customers. Exceptional customer service means more than making the customer happy today: It means making that customer a customer for life! Being willing to go the extra mile with your customers will keep bringing them back. Being consistent in product quality, in continuous improvement, in demonstrating outstanding, outrageous customer service, in educating and inspiring employees, will make your business soar.

> "The secret of joy in work is contained
> in one word - excellence. To know how
> to do something well is to enjoy it."
> - Pearl S. Buck

Patience, Patience

Once, when I was attending a conference, I stayed at a hotel for several days in a row. Whenever I left or returned to the hotel, I noticed a janitor, happily working. He was always, very methodically, sweeping the floor and because I am a student of human behavior, I couldn't resist asking him: "Don't you ever get tired of working all the time?" He flashed a huge smile at me and said, "I am an honorable man, and an honorable man keeps self-respect intact by always doing a good job." It reminded me of the old saying: "When the student is ready, the teacher arrives." He was really saying that you don't work for the boss – you work for the honor of maintaining and growing your own self-respect.

Some people work on their passion part-time for years because they have to work for money during the day. They go to school at night, or paint pictures all weekend, or get an internship that doesn't pay but teaches them what they need to know to succeed in what makes them happy. If, while pursuing what you love on the side, you maintain the attitude that any work is honorable if you do a good job, work can take on a purpose grander than just showing up and hoping to make it through the day.

If you can't leap with both feet into your passion, you can still find some satisfaction in doing the best job you can. Obviously, it's far more preferable to do something that you are passionate about, that's stimulating and challenging, than to spend your life doing a job you don't like extremely well. Let's get that out in the open – I don't intend to perpetuate the old lie that work is its own reward, because it isn't. *Passion for your work is its own reward.* It rewards you with more than a paycheck. People who are happier at work are physically healthier and tend to be emotionally stronger. When you do what you love, it opens the door to having a sense of calmness – including a feeling of rightness with the universe, an optimism and energy that goes beyond just having fun. It's a spiritual experience. You were put on this earth to do something important – to express the finest and most talented parts of yourself.

I know a woman who bought a rose bush for her tiny but much-loved garden. She was excited about this bush, as it was supposed to bloom with large, fragrant, peach rose-pink blooms. She planted it in a pot and kept it watered and fertilized, but it didn't do very well. It was always fighting an orangey mildew, its leaves looked sickly and dropped off a lot. She hung onto it for a year before it bloomed, and then it was a disappointment to her. The blossoms were almost scent free, tiny and red with few petals. They each lasted about one day. She wondered aloud how she had managed to buy such a crummy bush when the label had promised so much.

Then one day, she spotted something on the other side of the plant. When she turned the pot around, across from the homely, sad blooms, she discovered a large, multi-petalled, apricot-colored rose. It was the rosiest-smelling kind of tea rose, exactly what she thought she was getting in the first place. Her best guess was that the peach rose had been grafted onto another root – a common horticultural practice that weds hardy roots to more spectacular flowers. But the rose hadn't been pruned properly at the nursery, so the root stock grew canes too, and bloomed with the original flower. When she looked more closely at the plant, she noticed that the small red roses were growing on sickly-looking, small, yellow-leafed canes, but the leaves surrounding the apricot bloom were shiny, green, and fat. In effect, she'd bought two completely different roses on the same plant.

If you've ever known someone who was clearly meant to be a surgeon but was working instead as a third-grade teacher, you've seen an example of this error in purpose. When their true purpose isn't being expressed, people get mentally twisted and mal-nourished. They might look like they're surviving, but they aren't in proper bloom. The rose didn't have much choice – until someone pruned off the un-healthy canes to encourage the intended growth, it would keep putting out ugly flowers throughout its

life span. People have choices, though. What would you like to cut back, and what would you like to encourage to grow? Perhaps that's as much as I can get out of that analogy, but maybe that's all that's needed.

**"The sun does not shine for a few
trees and flowers, but for the
wide world's joy."
- Henry Ward Beecher**

Be Your Own CEO

A great way of building your confidence in your ability to create the kind of work life you need is to take personal responsibility for what happens in your lifelong career, not just this job or the next one. One of the reasons most people don't want to face the lie of the "get a good job, stay twenty years" story, is because it means the things we once could take for granted are things we can no longer believe in. Specifically, those things include company-provided health care, pensions, 401Ks, and insurance. You might have all those things today, but they may evaporate tomorrow.

The existentialists said it best: Freedom demands responsibility, and in this case, if you want to stay free of the perception that you may acquire security by hooking up body and soul with the "right" company, you need to be mentally ready to take care of your health, insurance, and retirement needs on your own. This may look like finding a community-based, sliding-fee health insurance if you're working for low pay (Kaiser Permanente has something called the Steps Plan that can start individuals out at under $50 per month for the first year). It may mean starting your own Roth IRA and contributing to it month-by-month like a savings account. It definitely means acquiring some sense of what happens to your money. It means giving up the perception that some company will take care of you. The sooner you give up the myth of the "nurturing" company, the less you will be affected by companies that disappoint their employees.

We are all entrepreneurs: the more joyful among us already see themselves that way. It is an existential crisis and as such, it brings up the terror of being totally alone with yourself in the work world. But once you confront the fear, map out a retirement plan, take care of your insurance issues, plan for your kids' education, you will feel at peace, confident that you are moving in the right direction. Robert Kiyosaki, author of *Rich Dad Poor Dad*, said that one of the things "rich dads" teach their kids is that, no matter who you work for, you also always "mind your own business." His point is that it's vital to consider yourself a businessperson in your own right so that whatever else you do, you attend to your own finances with the mindfulness of any CEO. When you accept the responsibility of becoming your own CEO, you gain confidence. After all, who better to watch

out for your interests?

As more and more of us start to see ourselves as entrepreneurs, the workplace will naturally change to accommodate our new perceptions. In some ways, that's already happening as more and more people work as consultants, or on contract. Mutual funds are being created for individuals, so changing jobs doesn't affect them; and some workplaces are providing benefits that are reminiscent of years gone by such as on-site day-care and health clubs to meet employees' needs for family interaction, and energy-boosting (medical-cost reducing) workouts. Companies that take the time to think about employees' needs want to attract employees rather than imprison them, and worker freedom and mobility is an important factor in keeping employers humble.

Your Inner Ecology

The most important factor in achieving joy in your workplace is your own inner ecology. Your inner ecology is the landscape of your mind and heart. If it's clear, well-kept, and clean, it's easy to see what matters most to you and to make decisions that reflect your personal values. The closer your decisions align with your values, the happier you will be. On the other hand, most of us have an inner ecology that's suffered the depredations of bad bosses, greedy companies, stupid policies, and inadequate pay. Our souls are junked up with old baggage; our hearts are wounded. I think we suffer as much trying to find the right work with the right colleagues as we do trying to find our life partners. We don't expect to be hurt by the workplace as we do in love, maybe because no one writes songs about it. But the workplace is too often a place of loss, fear, and pain. People abuse each other at work in ways we would never tolerate in our personal lives. And it takes a toll. We lose trust in the workplace as a viable opportunity for joyful interactions.

Your inner ecology is like any other environment: It can be cleaned up, purified, re-planted with positive ideas and solutions. But don't rely on other people to do this work for you – you are the only protector of your soul. Think hard about experiences you've had and from which you've learned. Observe your workplace and decide if it's worthy of you, and if you are contributing all you can to it. Throw out perceptions that hinder you, and try new ones. Think of yourself as an artist creating something powerful and meaningful.

Recognize Your Limitations

Some parents tell their kids, "You can do anything you want to do," and although it's a nice affirmation, it's not actually true until you back up what is really a wish with some tangible skills. Telling a child, "You can read," has little to do with the truth of teaching a child to read, and having the desire to read without actually acquiring the skills to do so is often known as "illiteracy." It takes alphabets and phonics and practice and working your way up from reading small words to learning bigger words.

Like reading, just wanting to have great work that you love isn't enough: You have to find enough motivation to take the classes, practice your art, study for the license, do whatever you have to, to make your dreams real. Sometimes recognizing your limitations can be painful. If I have heart trouble, I may have to admit that I'll never be able to learn to fly, even though I'd love to do so. Sometimes, you can be stopped by truth, but these times are rare. In general, where there's a will, there's a way. I might decide to take a personal risk and learn to hang-glide. Recognizing your limitations doesn't mean being stopped by them, not at all. It's where you start from to get to where you want to go!

**"You deserve the fun, the joy, the freedom, and the pure goodness that flows through the experience of love that indwells you... The choice is yours."
- David McArthur and Bruce McArthur, *The Intelligent Heart***

Screw Your Courage to the Sticking-Post

I think Lady Macbeth said this while planning a murder, but I like the sound of it anyway. Whether conspiring to mayhem or dreaming of a new career, to go through with your best-laid plans, you've got to have some way to control your fear. Fear is like a big dog, maybe a slightly slow-witted Saint Bernard, that hasn't been trained. Fear is protective, so that if you fear stepping in front of that moving bus, you are much less likely to end up as a blot on the asphalt. But fear, being unwieldy, can be unmanageable. If you don't manage it, it will take you for a ride.

> **"Courage is not the absence of fear,**
> **but rather the judgement that**
> **something else is more important**
> **than fear."**
> **- Ambrose Redmoon**

I know just telling someone, "Don't be afraid," isn't exactly therapeutic genius. Go ahead, be afraid. But *go ahead*. Fear and courage aren't opposites – heroes are people who behave bravely while experiencing terror. So recognize that you're about to make some changes, which are scary in themselves, and plan for the fear. Decide how much of your fear is realistic and how much is just superstition or a lack of confidence, and minimize your rational fears with careful planning. Find people who encourage you, and avoid the ones who prefer you to remain unchanged. Talk positively to yourself, and to others. Tear into the things that scare you most so you can see them for what they actually are – challenges you will one day master.

"We wise grown ups here at the company go gliding in and out all day long, scaring each other at our desks and cubicles and water coolers and trying to evade the people who frighten us."
– Joseph Heller, *Something Happened,* 1974

Chapter Three
Workplace Leadership
Connecting with Others

Labor, Management, and the Emotions

It's tempting to write a whole book about the relationship between management and labor, but I think it will serve a higher purpose to write about the things we all need – and need to demonstrate – in the workplace. Obviously, when management and labor find a way to treat each other with respect, there is a stronger basis for building trust. When leadership is firm, fair, and fun, the work environment is more conducive to honest interactions and reasonable expectations on everyone's part. It is my belief that leadership is a set of skills that can and should

be distributed throughout the organization, which also helps diminish the have/have-not atmosphere of too many traditionally-run organizations.

Trust and respect take time and grow over a history of honesty and good faith. To establish respect and a basis for trust, that history must be based on ongoing awareness and practice of courtesy, empathy, and anger management.

Courtesy

**"You must be the change you
wish to see in the world."
- Mohandas K. Gandhi**

If people were like machines, courtesy would be the oil that reduces friction and keeps things running smoothly. I wonder if the word "courtesy" is even something people relate to anymore, or if it just defines me as hopelessly old-fashioned: I like to think it doesn't! But whether or not my credibility is affected by offering up such an old-fashioned idea, I have to go on, because I know that courtesy is the heart and soul of creating and maintaining Synergistic relationships. People who can't treat each other, with respect expressed in mannerly interactions, can't trust each other. People who can't trust each other, can't achieve Synergy. It's that simple.

What may be less simple is bringing courtesy back

to a workplace that's been running on the smart-ass one-liner, the zinger, the substitution of mean-spirited jokes for meaningful discourse. Sniping at each other verbally is a compelling habit, and a hard one to break. It provides immediate (but short-lived) satisfaction, expresses some hostility, provides an on-going game that makes the workday more interesting if not more stressful, and meets the unhealthy "need" for competition between co-workers. It also creates animosity right and left, slows productivity, and demolishes morale. Because it is a habit, it's by nature not easily eradicated, but must be worked at with determination and zeal. Here are a few ideas for creating courtesy in your organization:

1. Teach manners and etiquette to everyone in the organization. Don't just expect people to know what good manners entail. People often don't teach their children manners anymore.

2. Hold manners classes, with activities and games.

3. Throw a semi-formal party to celebrate the end of etiquette lessons.

4. Expect senior members of the company to lead by example, and fine them for infractions. Donate the money to a peace organization.

5. Take a week or two and call each other "Mr." and "Ms." at every interaction. Then hold a meeting where people can

talk about what it feels like to speak to each other more formally. Encourage everyone to think of each other with the respect that titles bestow.

6. Teach team leaders and managers how to counsel employees who have been enemies.
7. Find a way to end the enmity or move the enemies apart in the organization.
8. Put up posters that read "Courtesy is Contagious." Have employees submit their own posters on the theme, and put them up, too.
9. Build courtesy into employee evaluations.
10. Make courtesy a core company value. Fire people who are unwilling to be courteous.

Empathy

> **"Since you get more joy out of giving joy to others, you should put a good deal of thought into the happiness that you are able to give."**
> **- Eleanor Roosevelt**

Empathy is what I experience when I put myself in your position and try to see things from your point of view. When I do this without self-consciousness or any other motivation beyond that of wanting to understand your experience, I can feel what you're feeling. When I empathize with you, I am not feeling pity for you: I am understanding what it is to be you, if only for a moment or two. And it's that moment that can change an entire relationship for the better.

I think empathy is an emotion basic to human consciousness. If, in a roomful of babies, one starts to cry, others join in. Maybe that's empathy! Research shows that when a mother is upset, her baby picks up on that feeling and starts to cry. Imagine! The tiniest person can feel what someone else is feeling and express it, too!

Empathy is the precursor to compassion. When we imagine someone else's trouble, we can feel that person's pain very keenly. And sharing someone's painful feelings brings us closer to them. That closeness nearly always results in wanting to help that person, in wanting good things for him, which is compassion. Compassion arises spontaneously from our awareness, and although I think we're born with the ability to empathize, I also think that life can change us, can cause us to shy away from empathizing with others. We may harden ourselves to empathy to protect ourselves from feeling other people's pain and from feeling responsible for soothing it. We may lose our capacity for empathy, or maybe I should say we lose our willingness to empathize, when other

people are cold to us, when they let us down. It's human enough, but sad to say, "Well, no one's done anything for me, and I'm certainly not going to do anything for anyone else. Why should I?" I think a lot of people end up losing their empathetic qualities because they've been hurt; they've been disappointed or betrayed.

The Scrooge Dilemma

In that old classic, *A Christmas Carol*, Scrooge is a perfect example of one who has lost the willingness to empathize. He could choose to understand the terrors of those around him, but he prefers not to. And in the misery caused by being totally alone in the universe, he begins to take a perverse pleasure in making other people unhappy: That does not mean it makes him happy. You see, that's the worst thing about giving up on empathy: It not only prevents you from helping others, but it causes you terrible pain. Helping others, as it turns out, is necessary to the health and well-being of the individual. Being helpful, demonstrating caring, strengthens the immune system, lowers the blood pressure, reduces stress, and makes us happy. When Scrooge dismissed the Ghost of Christmas Past as "a blot of mustard...a bit of undigested beef," he was using the primitive defense of denial to fend off awareness. When he could no longer prevent himself from seeing the terrible effects of his lack of compassion, when he began to see and understand and empathize with others, he began to change. He *had* to change!

Now, Scrooge was a hard case. His change wasn't really effected until he looked upon his own grave. The seeds were planted, but in the end it was the awareness of his wasted possibilities that made him decide to rejoin the living. And we discover the reason for his change from an openhearted young man to a selfish, heartless, old one. It was love that changed him. He had given his heart to a young woman who rejected him. When she disappointed him, he locked up his broken heart and decided to become fiercely successful and never be open again. It took the terror, sadness, and awareness and, finally, willingness of that Christmas night to return him to his original, loving, empathetic self. He realized that, unless he participated in the lives of others, his life was lost. He had to save others in order to save himself.

The workplace, we have been told, is no place for emotion. I'm not sure when that idea came about, but I'm guessing it was with the start of the industrial revolution, when workers moved out of farms and fields and into the noisy, mechanized factories by the hundreds of thousands. Maybe there was something about the grandeur of all those machines that made people want to function like them; smooth, quick, with the only problems being obvious, mechanical needs. Wouldn't it be nice if all we had to do to improve morale or productivity was to replace a belt or tighten a bolt? Maybe this wish became translated into the idea that emotions have no place

at work. It's a silly idea: Where people gather, there will always be emotions. The main question now is, how can we maximize the good, useful feelings and minimize the harmful, hurtful ones?

Empathy and compassion are vital to our happiness. The Dalai Lama's message in *The Art of Happiness* returns again and again to the necessity of compassion in our lives. And it's important to realize that when it comes to compassion, there is no such thing as status or power or any of the things that may divide us in the workplace. When the Dalai Lama has concerns about the state of the Tibetan government, he says he is likely to share those concerns with the person who is sweeping his floor. After all, that's the person he sees when he returns to his room. And the person sweeping your floor is at least as likely to be able to empathize with you as the head of state sitting downstairs in the conference room.

Compassion has two parts. So far, I have focused on the internal part, the empathy that gives rise to the feeling of compassion. The second part of compassion is taking helpful action. When Scrooge regained his room on Christmas morning, he didn't just sit around feeling good about all the things he had learned about himself: He immediately set about changing things for the better. Real compassion naturally creates some sort of action, and someone who says they "feel for you," but who does nothing about it, probably isn't experiencing compassion.

In a compassionate workplace, problems that are

affecting people become causes for action. A business owner in Southern California ran his company in an old-fashioned way in that he felt responsible for his employees' well-being. Most of his employees were also commuters and at some point, it came to his attention that many of them were leaving home at four-thirty in the morning in order to make the trip on time. They weren't eating breakfast, either, and so by the time they got to work, they were exhausted and hungry. He took direct action by building a cafeteria and making sure everyone who worked for him had breakfast once they got to work. When he found that employees' health needs weren't being met, he hired an on-site nursing company who could talk with the workers, dispense basic medicines and advice, and refer employees to the doctor for more serious health problems. By these two actions, the president took care of his employees' health in a common-sense and preventive manner. He demonstrated his compassion by action and was rewarded not only with better productivity and morale, but with the appreciation of his employees and the satisfaction of taking care of his people. Moreover, this company continues to be a highly profitable, much sought after place of employment.

Honesty

"It does not require many words to speak the truth"
- Chief Joseph

Without honesty, it's difficult to practice compassion or to give and receive empathy. In the example above, the company president had to be able to admit to himself that his employees' needs weren't being met and that it was his responsibility to meet them. Otherwise, he would have done nothing, and everyone would have suffered. Still, many employers would rather let everyone suffer than admit to themselves and to others that their current company management isn't perfect.

When we are honest, we don't have to pretend to possess an expertise we don't really have. We don't have to try to impress each other. Being honest with oneself is a great guide to peace of mind because we can assess our limitations with a sense of reality. As I said earlier in the book, when I know my limitations, it's harder for me to create unrealistic expectations. When I don't expect unreasonable things, I'm not going to be disappointed as often. When I'm honest with myself, it's easier for me to be honest with you.

It's difficult to feel much compassion for someone who isn't honest with us. In fact, being honest with each other may be one of the most basic human courtesies. When someone fails us in honesty, we respond by removing our trust.

I know a therapist who sometimes saw walk-in clients at the college counseling center where she worked. One day, a young woman came in because she was upset by something her boyfriend had done. When the counselor started talking with her, the client told her that she was angry because her boyfriend had openly cheated on her with another girl.

The counselor empathized with the young woman and tried to understand more deeply what she was feeling. But that didn't last long, for in a few minutes, the client told her straight out that she had cheated on her boyfriend and told him about it; twice! He had been upset, but he loved her and had taken her back the first time. The second time she told him she had slept with someone else, he went out and did it, too, then told her about it for revenge. She felt no guilt or remorse over cheating on him: What she couldn't understand was where he got the nerve to do the same thing to her!

Right about that time, the therapist had what professionals euphemistically call a "failure of empathy." How could she feel sorry for this girl who obviously didn't give a damn about anything but her own wants? Why should she empathize with someone who had repeatedly hurt another? Now, the mature part of herself told her that in these cases there is nearly always more to the story: perhaps the young woman

had been hurt before, or perhaps she was raised in a hostile family. Maybe she was purely a sociopath and had no conscience, in which case it would take a very special sort of counselor to work with her. There are almost always reasons why people act selfishly, without concern for others, but it takes time to discover those reasons.

The struggle for the therapist was in feeling direct empathy and compassion for someone whose problem was deceit. For the problem as it was expressed – "My boyfriend cheated on me!" – she could muster no compassion. For the underlying problem, that this client was incapable of having a trusting, intimate relationship, she found a well of compassion. You can feel real dislike for someone when meeting them in a superficial way, but once you start to dig, there's almost always a place deserving of your compassion.

At work, especially in places where emotions are expected to stay underground, we may have a tough time finding compassion for each other. In many workplaces, our true selves wear armor of defensiveness, image, status, "professionalism." It can be difficult to see behind the defenses to the core self, the self that inspires empathy and compassion. That's why I say that a healthy workplace allows people to be honest with themselves and each other.

Anger Management

**"Don't hold onto anger, hurt or
pain they steal your energy and
keep you from love."
- Leo Buscaglia**

Freud thought of anger as something that builds up and increases in pressure until its release, at which time the pressure decreases. It was called the "hydraulic model" and for a long time, people thought of anger as being a toxic fluid that should be encouraged to burst out. A neat way of conceptualizing one of the most powerful emotions, but when we decided that the way to release anger is to express it, we made a critical mistake. Anger, it turns out, is more like another of earth's elements – fire. The more you "vent" your anger, the more hotly it burns, until it eventually consumes everything around it. Like fire, it destroys relationships and can destroy the body, eating it up with cancer, hardening the arteries. If anger is like fire, it must be a little bit of hell on earth as it burns up empathy and compassion, reducing the spirit to ashes.

Researchers have found again and again that the seventies' idea of "letting it all hang out," while making for interesting fashion choices like the tube top, is not the way to handle anger. The idea that anger is a poison that can be expressed and "gotten out of your system" is incorrect: Studies show that expressing anger actually increases it! People who scream or throw things or hit others or say mean things when they are angry are likely to stay angry, and get even angrier. Like greed, anger is a parasite that feeds on its host's attempts to satisfy it. The more you try to get it out, the bigger it grows.

Why "Venting" Anger Makes It Worse
Venting your anger is like getting into a place on the freeway where you can't change lanes, so you can't get to the exit. You just keep driving down that furious road, getting further and further from where you want to be. In the seventies, psychology took a wrong turn in assuming that everything we feel should be shared fully and immediately with those around us. In fact, that works pretty well with positive feelings, increasing them in a positive feedback loop; where a smile creates happy speech, which fosters positive actions, thus making people happier. But it turns out that letting anger out creates a similar loop just as expressing the feeling in words strengthens the angry feelings that create harsher words and even angry actions. Anger tends to dissipate better when we count to ten, focus on something more positive, or try to understand what made us angry rather than just spewing venom at whoever's around.

The fact that anger doesn't operate hydraulically is another reason to encourage – to insist on – courtesy in your workplace. Discourtesy is an expression of hostility and starts the anger loop, both in the person who expresses it and the object of that hostility. In a sort of negative Synergy model, if I say something hateful to you, I have not only made you angry but increased my own wrath. Courtesy may not always stop anger, but it will stop it from growing and infecting others. It may sometimes even put a natural end to anger as people seek other ways to manage their feelings. Especially in relationships with troubled pasts, courtesy is an important precursor to empathy.

> **"Keep away from those who try to belittle your ambitions. Small people always do that, but the really great make you believe that you too can become great."**
> **- Mark Twain**

Competition – The Brutal Art

Akin to anger, competing with one another can cause unhealthy relationships in an organization. Ours is a culture that values competition for competition's sake, but it's time to unload that baggage. Competitive workplaces are stressful, filled with anger and scheming and unhappy people.

Certainly, you've heard the expression "Eat your heart out," which is usually said when we have just bested someone at a game, bought a fabulous car they could never afford, or stolen their sweetheart away. It is the expression of the winner over the loser. Not a graceful winner, not the kind of winner who takes you out for a beer afterwards and claps you on the back and says, "You'll beat me next time, then *you'll* buy the beer." "Eat your heart out," I suspect, comes from the ancient days when some tribes believed that the way to finish off a conquest was to rip out your enemy's heart and eat it. It was two things – a great way to make sure your enemy didn't come back to get you, and also a way to incorporate the courageous qualities of your enemy into your body (the word "courage" comes from the French for "coeur," which means "heart"). In a way, eating your foe's heart was an acknowledgment of his bravery – a sort of Bronze Age compliment.

When you tell someone to eat his [own] heart out, you're saying his heart lacks any quality you find worth keeping for yourself: It isn't even worth your eating; which, if it's true, means you were fighting below your standard. If he's going to wipe somebody out, a true warrior chooses a foe worth conquering.

"People who think – get in sync."

Competition Between Companies is Good Business

A foe worth conquering is not the guy in the next cubicle: He's the guy (or gal) in the company two miles down the road who wants that advertising account or architectural contract as much as you do. While competition between companies is the foundation of free enterprise, competition between individuals who work together is counter-productive. I sometimes wonder if people end up fighting each other in the same company because they forget that the real competition is out there, not in here.

When Southwest Airlines was trying to get off the ground, airlines who already had local markets tied up did everything they could to keep Southwest from getting started. They made it difficult, but they also made the folks at Southwest think seriously about creative ways to run a business when it seems like the whole world is trying to stop you. In some ways, the success of Southwest is partly due to the fierce competition they've endured (and triumphed over).

Competition with other businesses makes companies stronger, resulting in imaginative promotions, improved customer service, and consistently upgraded products. Honest competition between companies makes the business world go 'round! When I talk about negative competition in this book, I'm talking about competition between people who should be working together to achieve Synergy rather than inflicting the dog-eat-dog model on their colleagues and employees.

"The nicer I am, the more people think I'm lying."
- Andy Warhol

Dogs Don't Eat Dogs

It's funny that the concept of competition breeds expressions that involve ingesting one's opponent. We've all heard that "It's a dog-eat-dog world" but on reflection, I've decided that isn't strictly true. When someone says that it's a dog-eat-dog (DED) world, they are describing their personal world as either the Top Dog or the Hot Dog. If you want to work in that kind of world, you certainly may; and by your acceptance of its stupidity and the waste of your true talents, you will either feast on your opponents' entrails or have your own guts chewed up by ulcers. If someone higher than you in the company hierarchy conceives of the world as canine cannibalism, he or she will enforce that idea and make it true, and turn work into a feeding frenzy. If you are unfortunate enough to be higher in the organizational pack than someone with the DED mentality, watch your back. Or better yet, fire them.

The problem with the DED idea, aside from its repulsive hygienic implications, is that, eventually, even the vilest, most competitive, vicious cur will one day be beset by an up-and-coming mongrel with a taste for blood and high society. As the battle rages, everyone's attention is on the fight, while the things that really matter are just slipping away.

Competition within the company is not a viable model for workplace success, but it isn't going away overnight – paradigms take years or decades to shift. And competition is a large part of American culture: Americans don't like to lose. It's not genetic, but it's so deeply embedded in our cultural awareness that we can't seem to shake it. Although studies galore have found that classroom competition is bad for children's self-esteem and creates people who cannot work together, schools still use competition in grades, athletics, music, and drama. Scholarships are nearly universal in stating that they are "based on merit," not need. So it's natural that we would take this most unnatural of behaviors into the workplace. Competition is a great distraction. It's long been known by unscrupulous managers as a great way to keep the fighting between employees so that they can't band together against – you guessed it – unscrupulous management.

In fact, inter-employee competition is practically guaranteed to diminish an organization, to create conflict, communication blocks, lower productivity and create a hostile culture. If you are in a place where competition between colleagues is highly prized, all the energy that could be going into improving the company is being spent on politicking, backbiting, laying evil plans, and generally being unhelpful. The hostile atmosphere increases illness and absentee-ism, adding more costs to the company's debit sheet. At the very least, competition contributes to distrust and a certain amount of workplace misery. At the other end of the spectrum, we see bizarre events like the cheerleader's mother who murdered a competing cheerleader so her daughter could "get ahead."

Competitiveness is a defining characteristic of people – we organize our [sometimes unconscious] perceptions of people partly based on whether they are good winners or sore losers. Think of anyone you know, and even if you can't tell me his or her eye color, I'll bet you can tell me exactly how competitive that person is, and in what situations. Some people are tigers in the courtroom, while others can lose at Scrabble with grace and good humor. There are people who need to believe they are the best at everything, and others that just want to be the best at one or two things. Certain people will lie and cheat to win, and that "winning" seems as valid to them as winning honorably, but well-adjusted people don't care about besting anyone at anything – they just want to constantly better themselves.

What are your ideas about competition? Do you see it as a healthy and necessary part of your work life, or do you find it draining your energy and enthusiasm? If you think of yourself as someone who "thrives on competition," does that mean you usually win? Can you imagine your workplace with the intra-company competition removed? What would that look like?

The "necessity" of competing is a perception you might want to take a look at. It's a radical thing to say that competition between individuals is actually unhealthy, because so much of our culture depends on the idea of competition being a vital part of our much-treasured "rugged individualism." I think it's important to discriminate between the opportunity for productive competition between companies and the unnecessary and unproductive competition that takes place between individuals who are set against each other by the outmoded values of a dog-eat-dog corporation.

> **"The only competition worthy of a
> wise man is with himself."
> -Washington Allston**

When people work in a competitive organization, the imposed hierarchy becomes an obstacle to doing good business. People are so busy watching their backs and planning personal campaigns that company work takes a backseat to the individual's need to protect themselves. There just aren't enough hours in the day for both! Secondly, competition suffocates creativity. You don't want to be in the position of bringing up a new idea [that might fail] if co-workers are arm-wrestling for your parking space as soon as you open your mouth. Besides, new ideas are usually doomed to fail in a competitive organization because they serve nobody's purpose.

If you hear someone say, "That isn't my job," you may be in a competitive organization. In a place where hierarchy comes before getting the job done, people are resentful. They only do what they contract to do, and those who offer to do more are sometimes put severely in place by others who are threatened by enthusiasm that overreaches the job description. When someone says, "That isn't my job," they are saying so much more! This oft-used phrase can mean so many things, and they're all bad . . .

> I can't do it because I don't know how, and
>   I'm embarrassed to tell you that.
> I'm not supposed to do it because my boss
>   would be threatened by it.
> I'm not supposed to do it because I am a
>   woman, or a union employee, or
>   management, or an assistant, or the boss,
>   or (fill in the blank) _______________.
> I can do it, but I won't because I don't have
>   to.
> I'd like to do it, but I don't know how
>   because this company doesn't believe in
>   cross-training its employees.
> I could do it, but I don't like you, so I won't.
> I would do it, but if anyone found out, it
>   would be my neck.

I could do it, but it's Janet's job, and she
    would be furious if I stole her thunder.
I won't do it because I'm already
    overworked.
By asking me to do it, you are overstepping
    your authority to direct me.
By asking me to do it, you are imposing on
    my time.

Southwest Airlines hires people partly based on how uncompetitive they are. In group interviews, they look for people who are listening to and encouraging those who are giving five-minute presentations about themselves. The folks who sit there mentally revising their own presentations while someone else is speaking are not altruistic enough to fit into the Southwest culture, which prizes helpfulness above technical knowledge. And for those who still believe that only competition creates a winning company, Southwest Airlines posted consistent profits while other airlines went into gross amounts of debt or even out of business in the seventies and again in the nineties.

If you are a hiring manager, you might think about how applicants react to competition, because their competitiveness as individuals directly and negatively affects how well they will work in teams and how well they serve the customer. It also determines how political they will be, and how creative. If you are an applicant, you may decide to make one of the ques-

tions you ask at your interviews, "How does this company react to competition between employees?" The answer could tell you which will thrive the most – you or your migraines.

If you have some say in the way your company does things, you can implement policies that reward teamwork and remove competition. Arrange things so that people don't compete with each other; instead, they compete with themselves. You can't ask more than for your employees to do their best, and you should reward them for it. In the chapter on leadership, we'll address ways to reward people for their accomplishments.

If you are an employee in a place where employees don't have much say, there are still a couple of things you can do in regards to competition. First, if you've managed to land in a place where getting ahead means beating out other people (or being beaten out by them), you want to consider whether you might prefer to go someplace where more modern thinking prevails. Or, if you're pretty happy where you are, you may decide to take ownership by being helpful with others and becoming aware of those around you who are helpful to you. Building a network of people who value cooperation over competition is one way to positively impact the workplace. If enough people opt out of unhealthy competition, the corporate policies will (eventually) change to reflect the culture. Increasing communication between departments, celebrating company achievements together, and putting people from different groups together to work on agreed-upon tasks are all ways to reduce competition and increase trust between individuals.

There is a common philosophical idea of the "Other," which is opposed to the "Self," and in the workplace, the idea of the "Other" comes to its fullest meaning. Many organizations are quite hierarchical, so that you simply will not see the Assistant to the President having lunch with someone from the cleaning staff. The longer the leap in the hierarchy, the greater the Other's "otherness," or the more foreign people become to each other. At some levels, people stop thinking of each other as human beings with similar thoughts, desires, and capacities for pain. Like racism, hierarchism can be not just negligent but evil. The old strategy of having people trade jobs for a day is one way of decreasing otherness. Far better is to provide everyone in the organization with opportunities to cross-train, to learn more than they already know, and to prepare to move up. Otherness tends to disappear if we all share the same knowledge base, which is why in the best companies, employees at all levels are aware of industry trends, company stock prices, current strategies, and challenges. In a place where all are involved, there is no Other.

Synergizing with Your Customer

**"There is only one boss. The customer.
And he can fire everybody in the
company from the Chairman down,
simply by spending his money
somewhere else."
- Sam Walton**

A colleague of mine recently got into a rare shopping mood and went to a well-known West Coast department store. After dragging around a heavy bag from another store, she decided it was hampering her shopping experience and asked the clerk if she could leave it at the counter. The clerk hemmed and hawed and finally said, "We don't take bags from other stores. I guess if it's that heavy, you could get a cart." In the fitting room, another clerk was reprimanding a Korean woman who had brought her cart (with her heavy shopping bags in it) into her change room. "People need to get in here," snapped the clerk, apparently forgetting that her customer was "people," too.

My colleague, who is a customer service manager, was very irritated. She immediately reported the incident to the store manager who seemed completely disinterested. She decided to "vote with her feet." She put back the hundred and fifty dollars worth of clothes she'd been toting around and left the store without even a single swipe of her credit card. The tragedy for that retail outlet is that this one dissatisfied person told a convention of two thousand people her customer service horror story.

Clearly, the vibe at that department store was formal to the point of rudeness, and the concept of customer care, long dead and buried. In a shopping trip, it's easy to see what corporate values are being expressed on a day-to-day basis by the way the store is run, by the helpfulness of staff members, even by general store cleanliness. If you're thinking about working in a company that affords the possibility, check it out as a prospective customer. Look at its employees, its catalogs, its stock prices, its outlets and advertising methods. For example, one travel company put out an ad that showed a customer asking for extra peanuts on a plane, pocketing them, then reaching over to steal his neighbor's peanuts. The ad stated that he was "Our kind of customer – cheap." Is that the way this company conceptualizes what it means to be "cheap"? They approve of petty theft as a money-saving measure: Is that okay with you? Would you like to be their customer?

Communication is key in customer service, so while you're training people to serve external customers, you can also be introducing the concept of the "internal" customer, that is, the customer who is actually another member of the company. In a world where the most basic customer service has sometimes come down to some half-awake clerk saying, "We don't do that," the idea of using a customer service model of working with fellow employees may seem like the world's biggest joke. Assuming that the company has recognized the need for excellent customer service, the next step is to teach people that every single person in the organization is also a customer. When I am hired, I depend on the HR office to get my paperwork done in a timely way. If Payroll does its job, I'll get my first check on time. If not, I'll languish, as did a graduate student at the University of Illinois I once knew. The Payroll folks didn't get her paperwork done, and she didn't get paid for two and a half months. She had to take a second job in order to make the rent. She went to the Payroll office and talked and talked, but no one was interested in helping her get the paycheck she had already earned. You could say she was a dissatisfied internal customer.

There seems to be a lack of understanding when it comes to the importance of internal customer service. Success is really about building relationship bridges within the company (internal customers) so as to better build the relationships with external customers. It's an inside to out job. Companies that create employee profit-sharing plans help to make this reality more accessible by giving people a stake in the overall growth of the company. Employees can see in a direct way how their interactions with one another and customers affect the organization's profits.

If you are in a position to lead a company, the small, everyday decisions you make create impressions to the world at large about the way your company runs. From the janitor who does a spotless job day in, day out, to the executive team who run the boardroom, people in the company affect the way outsiders perceive that company. If you spend money on nothing else, spend it making sure that every employee is trained in teamwork, communication, and customer service.

Triple Win

Triple Win is just this: The employee wins, the customer wins, and the company wins. In a big, positive loop, employees who are well-trained and empowered will be invested in educating and serving the customer who will reward the company with continued patronage. A Triple Win culture is the reason customers keep coming back. Triple Win creates loyal customers who are very happy with the service, the product, and the company.

Triple Win is the reason for seeing your training dollars as an investment in your employees and company's growth rather than as a drain on profits. It's a simple yet powerful way to build a customer-driven culture from the inside out.

"Joy is the feeling of
grinning on the inside."
- Dr. Melba Colgrove

Chapter Four
Creating Zones of Inspiration

The most successful leaders (and by that I don't necessarily mean the ones with the multimillion dollar salaries, but the ones who lead profitable and honest enterprises, some of whom incidentally also earn multimillion dollar salaries) are interested in empowering the people who work for them. They aren't threatened by sharing information, by letting other people make decisions, and even taking control. They realize that the more that happens, the freer they are to focus on the big picture. I once knew a manager who said that if he did his job right, he hardly even needed to go in to the office: It would run along just fine without him. He was confident that the folks who worked for him knew what to do and if something that needed his attention came up, they were never afraid to call him for advice. It worked out pretty well: He started managing one location, then added another, then another. If he hadn't been able to let go of the little details, the company would have had to hire two or three additional managers to take on the new sites as they opened.

This chapter contains interviews with two Senior Executives of really fine companies. Each one of these leaders built an environment that allows employees to participate fully in the life of the company. Each one uses Synergy to push the organization to the forefront of innovation, while maintaining classic ethical standards of honesty, fairness, and mindfulness of purpose. Great leaders like these understand that their jobs entail freeing up people to do their best work. They see a positive work environment as a strategic tool that directly benefits the company. They also see employee education as a competitive advantage. Belief in the importance of their employees means that they make a commitment to the people who work for them. They don't see them as grist for some huge work-mill, but as the creative drivers of the organization. Smart leaders know that without supporting their employees, they would have nothing, so they use their own power to create Zones of Inspiration, places where trusting relationships exist and people are empowered to work without fear. Smart leaders have a knack for bringing Synergy into the workplace, and keeping it there. Here are some principles followed by these excellent Senior Executives. They:

*   Respect each individual and put that characteristic in the center of their philosophy.

*   Train managers in behavioral skills that go toward building a culture of integrity.

*   Are straight-liners – honest and open communicators, even when they are wrong.

*   Take care of employees, who in turn take care of the customers, who remain loyal and take care of their relationship with the company.

"Simple, clear purpose and principles give rise to complex and intelligent behavior. Complex rules and regulations give rise to simple and stupid behavior."
- Dee Hock, Founder of Visa

Interviews with Senior Executives

**Mick Pattinson, President, Barratt American, Inc.,
San Diego, CA**

Alexander:	Mick, you've been running Barratt American for a number of years. Tell us about your leadership style. What do you believe in?
Pattinson:	I believe in surrounding myself with good people, first of all, keeping those good people motivated, and leaving them, as much as I can, to do the job that we trust them to do. It's my job, as you say, to be the leader, to be out front, to set the game plan, to set the parameters, and to find the properties to develop and build new homes. And then let the key leaders do their job.
Alexander:	The idea that you're embracing right now at Barratt of exceeding customer expectations, could you elaborate on that?
Pattinson:	We believe that our job is to under-promise and over-deliver. We've set our goal of exceeding customer expectations. We want our customers to be satisfied with us every step of the way. We want the home-buying process to be as pleasurable, and indeed as thrilling, as it can be. We want the experience when they move into their new home to be enchanting; we want them to be satisfied with their new home for as long as they live there.
Alexander:	You want them to say, Wow!
Pattinson:	Exactly. If we can get them saying wow, then they will remember who made them say wow, and they will want to repeat that ex-

<table>
<tr><td></td><td>perience with us the next time they are in the market for a new home.</td></tr>
<tr><td>Alexander:</td><td>How do you go about making that happen?</td></tr>
<tr><td>Pattinson:</td><td>As the leader, it starts with the goals that we set for ourselves. We have set ourselves a goal to produce an outstanding, high-quality home every time we set out to build one. And in order to do that, it means everybody, at every level, has to raise their standards and their expectations. It doesn't just start with the salesperson; it starts long before that. The land we buy, the way we improve the lots, the design of the homes, the specification of the homes, the delivery process, the customer care after we deliver the home, everything has to be world class. And it's my job to surround myself with people who can do that.</td></tr>
<tr><td>Alexander:</td><td>You mean people that can pay attention to detail.</td></tr>
<tr><td>Pattinson:</td><td>Exactly. Pay attention to detail, not let any phone call go unreturned, not let any home be delivered with deficiencies when new homeowners move into a Barratt Home.</td></tr>
<tr><td>Alexander:</td><td>I know that Barratt American is one of the top companies in the California county areas of San Diego, the Inland Empire, and Orange County. Recently you received a lot of accolades and prizes in relation to that, right?</td></tr>
<tr><td>Pattinson:</td><td>Yes, we have received a number of awards from within our industry, not for just exceeding customer expectations, but for home design and for sales excellence, and that's an important recognition. We're proud</td></tr>
</table>

of that. We build homes throughout the Southern California region, and we take the view that customer care is crucial to our repeat business and to the success of what we do. We invest a lot of money every year into that aspect of our business. We have customer care professionals on every development, and past developments where we're no longer building, and it's a prime focus of what we do.

Alexander: I think more leaders should be creating symphonies of operational excellence. It appears that you don't mind individuals having fun, celebrating, and creating joy in the workplace. Is that true?

Pattinson: Oh yeah! We take the view, it's a cliché, but if you work hard and play hard, then you'll usually have a joyful, happy bunch. And a good happy crew . .

Alexander: Happy bunch . . .?

Pattinson: . . . yeah, it's what we're looking for. When people are enjoying themselves and they have a common goal, productivity goes up and costs come down. We also love to celebrate if we've had a good month. We'll meet in our company meeting room, and we'll have a party after work. I want people to feel that we recognize their hard work, and celebrating their achievements lets them know that everyone on the team has noticed their dedication. Whenever we open a new community, we'll have a big party and celebrate. When we win these awards that you refer to, we celebrate that, too. So we do look for opportunities to say to ourselves, and obviously to our associates that work with us, that we've done a good job and we've got something to be proud of; so let's be proud of it, let's celebrate.

Alexander: Job well done!

Pattinson: Job well done.

Alexander: Thank you very much. I appreciate your time.

Bob Evans, Service Manager, Fletcher Jones, Mercedes Benz, Newport Beach, CA

Alexander: Good morning, Bob.

Evans: Thanks, Chris, for having me.

Alexander: As you know, I've been on a mission of bringing joy into the workplace and at Fletcher Jones, you embrace certain ideas related to taking care of the customers and looking after your employees. Would you tell me about what you've done to date so that we can share that information with other business leaders?

Evans: We believe in under-promising and over-delivering and taking care of our customers as number one at Fletcher Jones. Customer care in the automotive industry has had a bad name through the years. So, our owner has always made that the number one item on his mind. With your help, we've been able to expand on that. Our challenge was the number of employees versus the huge amount of business coming. We service over 300 customers a day.

Alexander: Wow!

Evans: So trying to orchestrate that with over 100

	technicians, 21 service advisors, and a multitude of other people can be very exciting at best.
Alexander:	And very difficult, too. I mean keeping all the oboes and the violins and the bass players happy must be pretty difficult.
Evans:	It's a challenge. Some of them hit an off-note sometimes.
Alexander:	Right. Break a string or two.
Evans:	I try to let my people do their jobs, handle things as they should, and I'm there more to put out the fires and guide them when necessary.
Alexander:	So you're coaching and motivating and guiding as opposed to actually controlling everything.
Evans:	Absolutely.
Alexander:	So you decided that you're not the technician, that you're really the coach and leader.
Evans:	I want to be one of their team members with them, that's the important part; and you showed us that with Synergy: that the team approach was the important way to go.
Alexander:	Tell us more about that. How did you create more joy in the workplace for the customer, along with your team serving them from the inside out?
Evans:	Well, instead of having a shop of 100 technicians, we actually created small, individual shops of eight or ten technicians working as small individual groups of advisors.
Alexander:	You mean... you created self-directed work teams?
Evans:	Yes. They feel more empowered to make decisions in their own area. They don't feel

<table>
<tr><td></td><td>like they're part of a large body so much as they feel like they're part of a small team.</td></tr>
<tr><td>Alexander:</td><td>So, they have a say in the decisions that are made within that small team?</td></tr>
<tr><td>Evans:</td><td>Yes, each and every one of them do.</td></tr>
<tr><td>Alexander:</td><td>That's interesting. And so how did that affect the customer?</td></tr>
<tr><td>Evans:</td><td>Well, the employees felt a sense of belonging and became happier with the work environment and because of that, they do a better job. Their attitudes changed, and they weren't just out for the dollar, they're now out to make sure that the car is repaired properly.</td></tr>
<tr><td>Alexander:</td><td>Right. Because they have ownership.</td></tr>
<tr><td>Evans:</td><td>Absolutely.</td></tr>
<tr><td>Alexander:</td><td>Rocket science, huh? And so how did that impact the customer in relation to their service? If I was a customer coming in, what would I experience at Fletcher Jones?</td></tr>
<tr><td>Evans:</td><td>You'd be teamed with your service advisor, and that service advisor is teamed up with the technicians who would be taking care of your car. If necessary, they can talk directly with you, which is something a lot of dealerships do not allow. They have trouble with the customer being able to interact with technicians. At Fletcher Jones, we have that ability. We believe the customer is part of our family.</td></tr>
<tr><td>Alexander:</td><td>So in other words, you have one team always taking care of me?</td></tr>
<tr><td>Evans:</td><td>We always hope to have that.</td></tr>
<tr><td>Alexander:</td><td>And I would get to know that team?</td></tr>
<tr><td>Evans:</td><td>Yes.</td></tr>
</table>

Alexander: And when I came in, of course, the same service advisor, and so on.

Evans: That's our goal.

Alexander: So how did the whole idea of Synergy and the symphony of operational excellence help you? Was there one specific thing that you could say, 'this is what it did' - one specific thing that brought you joy, personally?

Evans: Well, just finding that the employees were happier. That made my life a lot easier and less stressful. I didn't have the whining and moaning that I used to have. I actually had smiling employees greeting me when they came in, in the morning.

Alexander: That's great, and that changed the whole atmosphere within the organization.

Evans: Absolutely.

Alexander: Right. Well, Bob, thank you very much for coming in and sharing your ideas with us and creating joy in the workplace.

Evans: Thank you.

> **"The labor of a human being is not a commodity or article of commerce. You can't weigh the soul of a man with a bar of pig iron."**
> **- Samuel Gompers**

The Harley Davidson Story

In 1981, Vaughn Beals and a group of executives led a leveraged buyout of Harley Davidson from AMF. It was the best thing that could have happened to this incredible symbol of American business.

At the time, Harley was dying a slow death, trying desperately to compete against Honda, Suzuki, Kawasaki, and Yamaha. Honda's failed inspection rate was only 5% against 50% at Harley. If you bought a bike from Harley, with your new owner kit came an aluminum foil pan to put under it, so that it wouldn't leak oil on your garage floor.

> **"We discovered that the key reason for our lack of competitiveness was poor management – by world standards – not U.S. standards. We were being wiped out by the Japanese because they were better managers."**
> **– Vaughn Beals, Chairman, Harley Davidson**

Rich Teerlink came aboard as President and CEO, and he began to rebuild the company from the inside out. He created the Leadership Institute to re-evaluate company goals and culture. He knew that

Harley was built on quality and customer care and needed to bring back the image of that quality for internal and external customers.

According to Ken Schmidt, a marketing executive and spokesperson, AMF's old mantra was to build and ship, build and ship, and it was this focus on the bottom line that took the company into what is now known as the Dark Era. Teerlink brought it out into the light – and as we all know – he succeeded.

The first focus was to increase quality through job enrichment and empowerment. Many employers had worked for Harley and knew how to improve quality without increasing costs, and now the leadership would allow them to perform. They did so magnificently, demonstrating extraordinary teamwork and customer responsiveness, and it was fun! Fun also permeated the marketing with many broader-based ideas such as "The Ladies of Harley" merchandise. Today this American symbol of capitalism and teamwork is an example for us all. A company is only as good as the best efforts of its people.

"True joy is that which gives us more energy and makes us feel more alive."
- Robert Puryear

Productivity and Joy

I first learned what it meant to experience joy at work, while at the same time working productively, when I became an employee of Curtis & Associates. Dean Curtis and Jeanne Ross, co-founders of the company, were masters at motivating their employees by having fun, learning new skills and growing professionally—all at the same time! Curtis & Associates was a small entrepreneurial company with just under 100 employees when I joined in 1993. I was fortunate to attend an all-company meeting in Nebraska two weeks later. The minute I walked into the room, I knew I had joined an incredible company made up of the most enthusiastic employees I had ever seen together at one time. The energy was bouncing off the walls!

Everyone at that meeting worked with people who were unemployed and on government assistance. They saw themselves as role models for the unemployed, which requires positive attitudes and an enthusiasm for working. Most of all they radiated energy, a love for life, and a passion for their work.

I soon learned that Curtis & Associates had regular meetings throughout the year so employees from across the country could share ideas and learn from each other. Every planned activity was energizing and fun with a learning component. Growing professionally was a structured process to encourage everyone to become the best at what they did, whether it was trainer, case manager, receptionist, writer, or marketer. Recognition of everyone's achievement by Dean and Jeanne was an important part of each meeting and an important part of the culture of the company.

I have taken the lessons that I learned at Curtis & Associates and use them to keep our employees motivated and to kindle a passion for their work. Regular team meetings are planned with fun and appropriate themes and always include team building activities to bond the group and make it easier to learn the responsibilities of their jobs. Employees, who enjoy each other, are happy to come to work each day, and are passionate about the work they do, will be a productive staff. This requires a time commitment from the supervisor, but it is the most important part of his/her job.

Helping others that are less fortunate to become self-sufficient and role models for their children can sometimes be a daunting task while at the same time can be very rewarding. Creating a joyful workplace where all employees jump out of bed each morning saying, "Yes, I get to go to work today" is a goal worth achieving.

- Dianne Owens, Regional Vice President, ACS State and Local Solutions—Workforce and Community Solutions

Lennar Corporation Culture

The culture at Lennar Family of Builders is the line of communication that drives performance consistency. The foundation of Lennar's culture is to have fun and to practice the "I Care" values. To a traditionist, Lennar may seem weird, quirky, maybe even strange: reciting poems, wearing badges, and having "Wow for Now" lunches and meetings.

As a speaker and workshop facilitator at Lennar meetings, I am impressed by the level of personal commitment and involvement throughout the entire corporation. Their culture is strong and trusting with a simple but very effective recognition program – "Wow for Now". The individuals selected to be recognized are those who have demonstrated to fellow associates, customers, or business partners that they practice the "I Care" culture values. Lennar is a highly profitable, value-led organization that rates extremely high on J.D. Power customer satisfaction listings. Once again, a value-led organization roars ahead, demonstrating that caring, fun in the workplace, and teamwork are powerful and acceptable strategies that really work.

> **"In times of joy, all of us wished we possessed a tail we could wag."**
> **- W.H. Auden**

"The very society of joy
redoubles it; so that, whilst
it lights upon my friend it
rebounds upon myself, and
the brighter his candle
burns the more easily will
it light mine."
- South

Chapter Five
Building Symphonies of Operational Excellence

By now, you probably have a good idea of whether or not you are willing to create joy in the workplace. If you don't want to, pass this book on to someone who would be more open to the idea. If you find yourself feeling optimistic, enthused, uplifted, or tickled by the idea of working in a joyful workplace, you may have already started implementing various ideas you've read about, and now you're wondering what to do next. So, here's what you do:

Create an Environment of Joy, Calmness, and Preparedness

No matter how hard we try to keep our homes and workplaces sane, sometimes craziness intrudes and we find ourselves trying to figure out how to handle crises. When conflict happens, as it will, redirecting negative energy towards solutions in a calm and common sense way will turn conflict into relationship building.

Avoid the old hierarchism model, which encourages a combination of secretive meetings and finger-pointing throughout the organization until the culprit(s) or scapegoat(s) are found and punished. Recognize how barbaric this system is: It may initially satisfy the instinctual, emotional urge for retribution, but it doesn't work well in the long term. The organization will falter in its purpose, while people are either avoiding or assigning blame. Buckminster Fuller said: "Real wealth is knowing how to direct energy."

Certain corporate cultures are calmer than others. Some are louder, more stressful, more frenetic. On particular days, an armed robbery would create less noise than lunch in the cafeteria. It's all in what you're used to! But even in the most hectic place, people who can keep their cool are valuable.

People can and should be hired for their coolness under stress, but it's hard to tell at an interview who's going to come through when weird situations arise. It's better to spend part of your training budget for preparedness. That might mean qualifying folks in first-aid; in others, it might mean managing a product recall with efficiency and sensitivity or learning how to handle an extremely irate customer.

> **"Life shrinks or expands in proportion to one's courage."**
> **- Anais Nin**

The heart of a fire fighter

The military cross-trains its people because many military situations are emergencies, and the more people who know how to fight a fire, the more likely it will be safely extinguished. There are all sorts of drills in order to reinforce that training with practice: invader drills, fire drills, rescue drills, bomb threat drills. Drills give people the chance to experience a situation before it's really dangerous: They come to know their own and others' reactions to emergencies. And when emergencies arise, people tend to do the right thing when they've had some practice at not only what to do but how to do it. Experience creates a sort of calmness of behavior that wouldn't otherwise be there. Anticipation is as important part of delivering quality service.

A business associate of mine described a situation that demonstrates the calmness that comes with experience on the part of the kitchen staff of a restaurant.

"I was once in a sushi bar when it was robbed at gunpoint. It was strange for me, in part because I was sitting with my back to the door and couldn't see a thing that was happening. The robber came in and shouted something like, 'Where's the money? Put it in the bag! Hurry!' No one said a word, not the hostess, the chefs, the patrons or wait persons. I didn't turn around to look at him (he was standing at the cash register, directly behind me). I didn't hear anything else until he was long gone. I was surprised at how quiet it was: On television, someone always screams when there's a robbery. In this case, it seemed the more intelligent choice was to stay quiet. The robber took the money and left; there was a long moment – maybe thirty seconds of total silence, then a collective sigh. I asked my dining partner, 'Is he gone?' then set down my teacup: It felt like I'd been holding it – and my breath – for a week. Then the waitresses began to cry softly and a few patrons got up quickly and walked out.

"I wondered how it was that nobody screamed or fainted (I nearly did faint, I was shaking so hard from not breathing). When the police arrived, I heard the hostess say that they had been robbed just a couple of months before: Their location was perfect for robbers because the getaway car could be parked and waiting at the gas station across the street. So the people at the sushi bar had some practice in being robbed!"

Aside from emergencies, a calm attitude at work (and at home) can avoid the effects of stress and the bad feelings that flow from it. A calm environment allows for clarity of thought and can make people feel more effective in their work. Courtesy and compassion help people to stay calm and centered.

Taken from Maslow's Hierarchy of Needs, Frederick Herzberg (The Herzberg Theory) talked about hygiene and motivational factors in the workplace. Herzberg claimed that it's necessary to satisfy hygiene factors before people can rise up to become self-motivated. Hygiene factors are such things as a good working environment – good supervision, recognition, and an opportunity to grow. He claimed if hygiene factors are not in place, workers will become demotivated. However, he also claimed that these same hygiene factors would not spur workers on to self-motivation, but, rather, that if hygiene factors were not taken care of, employees would become demotivated. Good working conditions in today's business world are considered to be the norm.

Choosing the right, soothing colors and comfortable work spaces, and knowing what is expected of you, is highly conducive of a balanced environment, which opens the door to expanded trust. To reduce anxiety at work, build a fountain with a few green plants and place benches where people can sit

and muse over the splashing water during lunch hour or breaks. Studies have shown that watching goldfish produces a calming influence, even significantly lowering the blood pressure. Many more companies are now providing lessons in meditation or deep breathing for people who would like to feel more centered and focused at work. They see the benefits immediately in employee efficiency and in long-term health care costs. All of these things can contribute to the quality of the workplace and the health of employees, letting people respond creatively and intelligently to unusually difficult situations.

> **"Either this man is dead, or my watch has stopped."**
> **- Groucho Marx**

Hire the right people

As I said earlier, you can't get anywhere with people you can't trust. Look for character and positive attitudes first – you can always train people in the skills they need. Be selective. Invest some time and effort into researching the kind of employee you value, and then find ways to attract the people you want to your interviews. Don't be cheap – interview more than once. Hiring is an issue of time, and you can invest it at the outset or pay later in attrition, firings, lawsuits, and general agony for everyone.

Market to everyone

Everyone agrees that marketing is an important part of running a company, but many people don't consider the importance of marketing to the internal customer base. You want your people to be excited about the products and services they provide. Marketing to your employees pays off in higher morale, increased product and company knowledge, and ultimately more sales. If I work for a company I believe in, I'm going to use their products, and I'm going to make sure the people around me know of their advantages, too. It's common sense! And it's a way of providing ongoing training.

Build your teams

When you hire the right people, keep in mind that you're not really looking for the bright, shining star who will make the company (or the department) run like clockwork. You're looking for people who can get along with others, who can communicate clearly and with gentility. You're looking for people who can be part of a team because when you're creating Synergy, you're using teamwork to get where you want to go. Building teams is more than just throwing people together and hoping for the best: Teams take more time to nurture, to smooth out the rough spots, and to come to an understanding that you really aren't interested in pitting them against each other in some sort of feudal competition for scarce resources. Team-building takes time, and you must be consistent in rewarding the whole team and encouraging the whole team to work together. Once people understand that you truly want them to work cooperatively, you'll be surprised at the quality of work they will produce.

**"The whole is greater than the
sum of its parts."
- Unknown**

Celebrate

People love to celebrate, and the rituals of celebration have long been used to mingle families and create goodwill between communities. Some dysfunctional companies have made the mistake of thinking that "celebration" is all they need to maintain enough employee cheer to get the job done. Workplace celebrations should be based on real achievements – they are meant to be a true expression of joy. Again, it takes a little more effort and more imagination than just instituting a casual Friday and then wondering why people are still dissatisfied.

In *Artful Work,* by Dick Richards, there is an excellent example of a celebration that was also a rite of healing. An entire department was dissolved, and when they met to discuss ways of ending, they came up with a solution that would address their hurt and enable them to say goodbye. The celebration turned out to be a funeral, complete with a Dixieland band. They buried their mascot, a teddy bear, and people talked and cried and hugged each other. It was a meaningful celebration: Those people were in the kind of pain that can't be touched by cake, which would have been an insult to their feelings. Formally and publicly acknowledging their distress was what the members of the department needed in order to move on to their new work with some degree of acceptance.

Celebrations should come from the heart, expressing the soul's desire to dance for joy. If you've ever watched a toddler get a present, you've seen that dance. It involves a big smile and arms that wave around like happy flags. It may be accompanied by stamping feet and sounds of delight. As we grow older, we formalize our pleasure with martinis and steak dinners, or put it off in favor of next month's trip to Vegas. The expression of joy, no longer spontaneous and unreserved, becomes rarer, more sedate. We might even completely forget what it feels like. But deep inside, where the toddler abides, we still long to dance.

Know Your Vision

**"All dreams come true, if we have the
courage to pursue them."
- Walt Disney**

It's important to know exactly what you stand for and what you intend to achieve. If you know what you want, the next step is to communicate it to everyone in the workplace. It's your responsibility to make your core values and expectations clear to people from the outset. When people know what's expected of them, they tend to meet and exceed those expectations. When they don't know, they flounder. Remember, you're also dealing with other people's backgrounds and baggage: It's entirely possible that at the last place they worked, they were expected to lie when cornered, blame others, compete viciously, and pad their accounts. Knowing and communicating your vision is key to setting ethical and practical standards in your workplace.

The responsibilities of a Synergistic leader include initiating the creation of a vision statement, the clarification and statement of values, and the choice of organizational goals. Using the vision, values, and goals enables you to create your mission statement. The mission statement has two parts: an internal statement that is motivational and energizing – a roadmap to success – it is the constitution of the business. The second part is a shorter, external statement that serves to explain, in a more general way, the purpose of the organization to the public.

The vision and values statement for the company may be an amalgam of individual vision, values and goals, and mission statements created by every individual on your team. Individual statements can be used to create team and department statements, which can be used for the end products – the corporate statements. Including as many people as possible increases individual empowerment and involvement. Involving everyone is important in ensuring that the majority of the company will buy into the organizational mission statement.

Use the checklist below as a guideline for creating your statements. It will help make certain that your visions, values, goals, and mission statement are appropriately aligned. It is the sheet music that is the first step to building a symphony of operational excellence.

Vision Checklist

1. Is the vision realistic?
2. Does it take all possibilities into account?
3. Is the vision a good fit for the culture, leadership, and style of your business?
4. Is the vision aligned with the values and goals of the organization?

5. Does the vision allow for an ever-growing and changing world?
6. Does the vision take all the organization's potential for accomplishment into account?
7. Is the vision inspiring and uplifting?

**"These are my principles, and if you don't like them, well . . . I have others."
- Groucho Marx**

An expectation meeting with Tony Bourdain. Anthony Bourdain, chef and author of *A Cook's Tour* (a great book and a terrific Food Network TV show), made a worldwide tour sampling the finest and weirdest of offerings, from the French Laundry in California to bags of crunchy fried insects in Bangkok. He ate scary things in Cambodia, traveled by motorcycle and camel and sampan. His attitude was key to the success of the show: The guy loves food with a passion that makes pure love look silly! In pursuit of food, Tony Bourdain, I am convinced, would do anything. In his book, he gives us a taste of his vision, values, and goals in what I would call an "expectation meeting" with a new sous-chef. He takes the new guy out to a bar before the official offer and acceptance, and he makes a little speech a-la-Godfather. It's a little rough talk, but he is a New Yorker and a chef, and his clarity of vision and dynamic communication style are stunning.

"I say, 'I'm the nicest, sweetest guy in the world. You call me at four o'clock in the morning needing bail money? I'm there for you. I'm not going to be riding your ass like some other chefs will. I won't humiliate you in front of your crew or anybody else. You don't have to address me as "Chef" all the time. I've got a sense of humor – and in my off-hours, I'm a depraved, degenerate animal – just like you. You will like working with me. We'll have fun...But if you ever screw me, talk shit about me behind my back, drop the ball, show up late, or show disloyalty in any way, I don't care if you're my dearest friend, I don't care if you saved my life, I will fire your sorry ass like I'm blowing my nose."

Tony Bourdain is clearly a bad boy: He drinks, he smokes, he uses bad language. He wears T-shirts with the sleeves cut off. But he uses good grammar, he reveres a fine sauce and writes a heck of a good story. He's a living example of a man who does what he likes to do, and he does it very well. He knows that expressing his vision requires hiring people who share his values, who speak his moral language.

"I feel that if a person can't communicate, the very least he can do is to shut up."
- Tom Lehrer, *That Was the Year That Was*

Attend to Your Values

**"He who stands for nothing,
falls for anything."
- Unknown**

Notice that one of Tony Bourdain's values is punctuality. If you need him to bail you out, that's fine, but you'd better not be late for your shift! Restaurants, more than many other businesses, exist to fulfill customers' needs in a most timely manner – a matter of minutes. Your values should be a part of what people know about you: They should be reflected in the way you do business. If you think it's wrong to kill animals, you are not going to sell furs in your business, even if someone very rich asks you very nicely. Whenever you can, be explicit about your values, especially when you're hiring, so there's no confusion. Spend some time thinking about what really matters to you – your values affect your goals. Maybe your work doesn't require people to arrive at eight o'clock sharp, and maybe you don't care when they come in as long as they do their work. In that case, your values in regard to punctuality may not be as strong as those revolving around honesty or tenacity or tidiness, or whatever. Basically, the more people understand what's important to you, the more likely they will be to meet and exceed your expectations.

Writing Your Value Statement

1. Values are about the ethics of your business – the reasons you want to do business.
2. Values must be clear and acceptable to your whole team.
3. The organization must be able to live up to them.
4. They must be clearly displayed for everyone to see.
5. The leadership must be able to "walk the talk."

Maintain Watertight Integrity

**"Truth never damages a cause
that is just."
- Mohandas Gandhi**

I want to talk about integrity here because it is a core value of mine, and probably most people. "Watertight integrity" is a nautical term: It refers to the internal structures of a vessel (such as ports and hatches) that can be sealed to prevent the flow of water into the ship. I like the phrase because in my mind it fits people, too. Personal integrity, like watertight integrity is not variable – either you have it or you don't. Having a little integrity is like being a little bit pregnant – impossible.

There's an old saying that a man's word is his bond. Deals between honorable people have always been settled and struck with a handshake, and neither party would think of reneging. If you find either a boss or an employee whose honesty you are certain of, you have the most important basis for an excellent working relationship. Software skills, leadership skills, even manners can be taught and learned. But integrity of the old-fashioned kind is a personal characteristic that either forms in childhood or not at all. It doesn't matter how well-trained or knowledgeable someone is if you can't rely on his or her integrity. It seems strange to have to say this, because it's completely obvious that honest colleagues are preferable to lying, disingenuous snakes, but consider whether integrity-related questions even make it into the interviews you've attended or arranged. And how do you write a resume that indicates integrity along with sets of skills or completed projects? How do you know when you interview at a company whether the people you'll be working with can be trusted with your talents and potential? With your heart and soul, really?

Interviewing is a bit too much like dating: You don't really know what you're getting until much further down the road. A boss who seems like a "nice person" after one or two interviews may tell you a few months later that he wouldn't hire a woman if he thought she might be pregnant, or a man if he thought he was gay. There's no way to tell for sure, although it's possible sometimes to talk with current employees (preferably away from the office) and get a sense from their behavior and stories whether honesty and fairness are considered important qualities in that workplace. Interviewing a prospective employee is also risky – someone can make a great impression at two or three or four interviews, and still not be right for the job. But if you have evidence of that person's integrity, you have a good start.

Integrity is also the most important quality in determining who's going to be a good leader. Leaders have to be trusted, and to be trusted they have to be the kind of people who will do what they say. It's a pretty simple formula, but one that some folks have a hard time grasping. "Wouldn't it be much easier for me," they think, "if I could just tell other people what to do and then scare them into doing it?" People who think like that have no place in leadership because they can't be part of a team. No self-respecting employee is going to work hard and take risks for someone who grabs the credit without doing the work.

A poet, scholar, and animal trainer named Vicki Hearne wrote a book called *Adam's Task: Calling Animals by Name*, which talks about the reasons for training dogs and horses but more so about the ways animal and human consciousness intersect and the ways they diverge. She tells a story about a police dog, a Doberman, who was working with his human partner when the policeman decided to take out his frustrations on a young woman he had stopped for

jaywalking. The policeman was beating the woman with his nightstick when the dog, "his" dog, attacked him. The Doberman removed the nightstick from his impulsive partner and stopped what he (the dog) recognized as dishonorable behavior. A dishonest department would have put the dog down for "turning vicious," but this story ends with the increased ethical education of the cop. This is just one tale, but there are hundreds of examples of the things we can learn from animals, many of which are about making moral choices at work.

Choose Your Goals Wisely

Goals should be specific. It's silly to make a goal of "doing better next year." That could mean anything! Quantify your goals and specify timelines. Goals should be achievable but not too easy. Goals set the tempo of your organization and challenge the people in it to do great things. A company in pursuit of its goals is a vibrant place to be!

Goals should have meaning for more than just the senior echelon of an organization: The more people who are excited and motivated to reach a goal, the easier it will be achieved. Tying individual rewards to corporate goals is a good way to motivate people at all levels of the organization. It takes a little more planning, but the payoff is company-wide. It's Synergy at work!

"2% of the people initiate, innovate, create, and make things happen; 14% criticize and condemn them and/or assist the 2% while they're making things happen; 84% don't know what's going on, because they don't understand the importance of setting goals."

Six Critical Factors in Goal-Setting
Goals...
1. Must have a timeline within which to operate.
2. Must be realistic.
3. Must be challenging.
4. Must be written down in detail.
5. Must be clearly communicated.
6. Must be aligned with your mission.

Once you have chosen your vision, values, and goals, it's time to build your mission statement. This is an opportune time to focus on Triple Win, as you create promising possibilities for employees, customers, and, of course, the company. This is also an excellent opportunity to use Synergy, listening to the opinions and needs of the people involved. If you begin your transition to Synergy by being open with others, by expecting and valuing input, by letting everyone take responsibility for their relationship to their work, you will also be creating trust and team-work as you "walk the walk" of Synergistic leadership.

Train Your People

Synergistic leaders must be ready to educate, to focus on training as an investment rather than a cost, and to expect that people will sometimes make mistakes. When you run into the occasional employee who will not work, who prefers to play games or be lazy, you must be ready to fire those who aren't living up to their responsibilities. Applying FAD (Fanatical Attention to Detail) means teaching those around you to take notice of the small issues as they arise, preventing them from becoming large issues. Please don't mistake FAD for micro-managing: FAD is positive, proactive, and founded on the question, "How could this be improved?"; micro-management is negative and reactive, based on an unhealthy need for control. FAD is about taking pride in one's work by attending to details with care and dedication. Small, continuous improvements can add up to big, important changes. Taking care of the small stuff means taking care of the big stuff, too; it's much easier on everyone involved if they are taking baby steps rather than making giant (and anxiety-provoking) leaps.

Have a plan. Every company should have a plan

of action for emergencies. Plans need to be tailored to the organization, as the possible emergencies of a sushi bar will differ from those of a data-mining corporation. Training at all levels should include emergency plans, and employees should be trained until they feel confident in carrying out those plans. In fact, emergency preparedness is an area where employees can help pinpoint possible emergencies and solutions. But there are some general guidelines everyone can follow when faced with emergencies.

Your Basic Emergency Plan

1. *Stay calm.* Panic only makes things worse. Breathe deeply and assure yourself that things will be all right.
2. *Do what has to be done.* If water is pouring through the hull, you don't have time to reason too many things out. Solve the immediate disaster and leave the rest until later.
3. *Take your time when you can.* Think about what needs to be done. Don't act just to react.
4. *Don't succumb to analysis paralysis!* The purpose of having a plan is so you don't get stuck in decision-making snafues during critical times. A good plan should prevent analysis paralysis.

5. *Focus on what's right.* Emergencies test our core values. Others may be expecting things from you that aren't yours to give. Think about the things that really matter before making a decision.
6. *Talk with those whose opinions you trust.* Don't let hierarchy or fear prevent you from getting the best information available to you.
7. Implement a plan of action, measure the impact of the plan, adjust, re-implement and follow through.

"What gets measured, gets done."
\- Unknown

"Gratitude helps you to
grow and expand;
gratitude brings joy and
laughter into your life and
into the lives of all those
around you."
- Eileen Caddy

"When you focus on the
strengths and not the
weaknesses of others, you
build trust and respect."

Chapter Six
Building Trusting Relationships

The rules for creating Synergy may look too easy, but they're based on letting go, and reevaluating the benefits of participation and idea sharing. Letting go is almost impossible for some people – either they don't feel comfortable with the coaching role, or they believe they can do it better – so why waste time?

1. (Anti-Trust Argument) People will not work productively unless they are forced to.

   (Synergy Argument) If people have to be forced to work, there's something wrong with the work.

2. (ATA) If I let them, my employees will
   rob me blind.
   *(SA) If you let them, people will make you a
   fortune.*

3. (ATA) If things go too smoothly, I may be
   seen as obsolete.
   *(SA) Things have never, in the history of
   the world, gone that smoothly.*

4. (ATA) If I don't make a decision, it may
   not be made right.
   *(SA) Sometimes even you will make
   mistakes. If you make all the decisions,
   you are teaching your people not to
   think.*

5. (ATA) If someone makes a bad decision, I
   will have his/her head.
   *(SA) If you punish your decision-makers,
   you will prevent the company from
   growing.*

It's been confirmed by scientific studies: People don't like change – it upsets them. Studies on stress have shown that even positive changes like inheriting wealth or being promoted can raise stress levels as much as negative events. CEOs are making changes every day. The recent corporate scandals have brought about the need for change. They can't get rid of their critics within the company, and they can't ignore the external critics any longer. Synergy has become a necessity. The rules for creating Synergy are simple, but they may require some real changes. The changes are worth it – the CEOs who have contributed to this book have proven that building Synergy builds long-term profits.

But each one had to first come to terms with the fact that creating a workplace based on Synergy requires some unusual understanding of the way people operate. Emotional understanding. In this book, you will encounter words that rarely come up in a MBA program. Words like "fear" and "pride" and even "sadness." Touchy-feely stuff that hard-nosed businessmen and women have traditionally scoffed at. I've heard it referred to as "software" – those mysterious emotional/limbic programs that run inside all of us. I've even heard people say that talking about feelings is "soft," and that no one is interested in feelings when discussing business. But when you look at the Internet and listen to people talk about their work, it's obvious that they are in pain, and that pain is costing them their health. And to any hard-nosed types out there who think that people should toughen up, suck it up, and get on with their work, those attitudes are costing you money: cold, hard cash that's being eaten up in sick days, mental health days, quitting, showing up but not getting the job done, even sabotage.

So, imagine me as a tough-talking drill sergeant whose mission it is to teach hard-nosed businesspeople the realities of working with people. We are *all* "soft." We are, in fact, about 90% water, the softest stuff around. So, toughen up, suck it up, and get on with the business of learning something about human software. And stop making excuses because you're afraid to deal with your own emotions. What are you thinking? Do you think motivation is a logical left brain process? If so, you're wrong. It's emotion, desire, aspiration, and dreams. Trying to build high performance without understanding and taking into account the emotional reality of the people in your organization is about as useful as trying to run a computer without software. So, buckle down and prepare for the rough stuff: the nuts and bolts we all need to be fully engaged (and happy) at work.

Trust

"Our distrust is very expensive."
- Ralph Waldo Emerson

People need to rely on each other to make ethical decisions, to stand up for what's right. Leaders who try for Synergy when they haven't yet built trust within the company are kidding themselves because people can't work wholeheartedly while they're busy defending themselves. Leaders can't be effective if they don't trust their teams, and team members can't be effective while jockeying for position, struggling for dominance, or spying on each other.

It is popular for companies to use a variety of experiential training to help people break down fear and build trust. The idea is that teamwork and trust are generic behavioral skills that can be learned. Crossing a ravine or climbing a wall on a rope can bring people together and ultimately accomplish what the work environment might not. Those experiences foster closeness for a time, but once is not enough. Unique experiences can sometimes bring about epiphanies, but when they are isolated events, they may not provide more than a few weeks or months of smoother working relationships. Feelings do wear off unless followed up by real and lasting changes in the workplace.

Unfortunately, it's not enough to simply decide to trust someone because we "have to" or in order to "be fair." Invariably, we have to take into account the other person's status in relation to us, power over us, and innate trustworthiness. People who were abused as children are notable for being willing to "trust" someone who is clearly untrustworthy. Ordering someone to "trust" you is a classic sign of an abuser, who relies on inspiring fear in others in order to control them.

You may believe in the other person's potential as a human being, and you may feel compassionate towards them. But trust should never be uncondi-tional – it has to be earned. Some senior executives actually believe that their position in the company mandates the trust of their employees. This is an interesting example of a warped perception leading to a bizarre sense of entitlement: "Trust me, or I'll fire you!" they roar through clenched teeth. And sane people, recognizing that behavior as morally uncon-scionable to the point of deviance, run like hell.

If someone is untrustworthy, power and control are the next considerations. If the untrustworthy person has power over you in the organization, you may need to find a more suitable occupation. If the person is someone employed by you, you need to find a new employee. Being trustworthy isn't like having a set of skills that can be trained into a person's repertoire: Being trustworthy is a state of one's char-acter, and by the time we start working for a living, that character is pretty much fully formed. I suppose it's possible that an unhealthy workplace can cause people to become untrustworthy but, in general, I would say that character remains the same across situations.

If you hire for character and train for skills, you'll have a good chance of establishing a workplace filled with trustworthy people. Gaining the trust of others takes time. People test each other, sometimes unaware that that's what they're doing. As a leader may give a team member greater and greater respon-sibilities over time, co-workers give each other chances to do right or wrong. Sometimes they'll ask one another to do wrong, and while it may foster a sense of camaraderie for a time, it wears away at the respect people would otherwise feel for one another. Stephen Covey, author of *7 Habits of Highly Effective People*, discusses the importance of knowing what your values are and understanding your principles. If you value honesty and your principles are based on acting honestly, you know how to answer another employee who asks you to clock in for her as well as knowing how to answer the boss who demands your support for decisions you know to be wrong. If, on the other hand, you value being liked and your principles revolve around pleasing whoever's around at the time (and a lot of people, through fear or insecurity, have these values), your answers will change with the situation. Reputation follows, so that some people are known for being willing to do anything for approval: They lose the respect and trust of those who know them. People who do what they believe is honest may not always be liked, but they will more likely be respected. Most important, they will be able to respect themselves.

In a scene from the romantic comedy *Moonstruck,* a neglected housewife eats dinner with a man she met at a restaurant. Afterwards, he walks her home, and when he realizes that the house is empty, asks if he can come inside. He is handsome and charming, his intentions are clearly romantic, her husband is cheating on her, the house is empty, and she would never get caught if she said yes. But she says "No," and when her chagrined suitor asks, "But why?" she answers, saying just this: "Because I know who I am."

The blandishments of a handsome man were mere distractions to this character: She would go on being who she was. And in a "silly little movie," we have a statement that is not silly, but is one of the most important lessons life can teach: You have to know who you are. When you know, really know, what matters to you, your actions mirror your beliefs. Your self-respect will not be swayed by external events. Other people may distress you, may even cause you harm, but you have something so solid to hold onto that you cannot be swayed into making stupid decisions, even attractively stupid decisions. There is a marvelous comfort in knowing who you are.

Victor Frankl, author of *Man's Search for Meaning,* found that knowledge in the hellishness of a concentration camp. People who had every reason to believe in their imminent death found reasons to live, found ways to care for one another. In a situation designed to bring out the worst in humanity, they found the finest in themselves. These people, strong spirits in tortured bodies, put their energies into being good to one another. Their focus was outward and positive and helpful. In the midst of a living nightmare, they still knew, or maybe knew even better, who they were.

Sharing

If the foundation of Synergy is trust, the essence of Synergy must be sharing. Synergy is experience, and we can't truly share the experience if you're shoveling while I watch. By the way, sharing got a bad name somewhere along the line. Sharing *isn't* about telling each other all our secrets and weeping in each others' arms: It's about working together to make things happen; taking the good with the bad. It's also about input – making sure team members have the chance to voice concerns, ideas, and suggestions that will help the job go easier.

We don't have to do the same job, but there has to be equality in the energy and investment we make. And if we screw up, we share the embarrassment, the remediation, and the rebuilding. Ideally, sharing should start at the beginning, with everyone involved in the project in on the decision-making and planning, so there is shared emotional investment from the get-go. In fact, Synergy runs on energy, and the energy of beginning a project is powerful and motivating – you want everyone in on it!

Contentment vs. Greed

**"Materialism originates from
thoughts of fear, scarcity, and
discontentment; thoughts
of abundance originate from
the idea that there is enough for all."**

There is a strange idea in our culture that contentment comes (with luck) sometime after retirement. I don't think that's necessarily true because hard-driven men (and increasingly, women, too) often drop dead soon after retiring, as if not having to strive anymore stole away their only reason for living. Most of us have moments of contentment, but we don't expect it to be a frequent part of our lives. In fact, I think that we associate contentment with a sort of emotional laziness: If you're happy with the way things are, you are unlikely to change them, and we do value change. It seems like, in business and in our personal lives, we're always on the lookout for ways to do things faster, cheaper, and more efficiently. We say, "time is money," and once you take that as your motto, it's impossible to feel content because time is limitless! In theory, something can always be done a bit faster, right? And we get used to advances in speed, to the point where units of time that are imperceptible to human beings are used as a selling point for computer hard drives.

When trains first came into being, people believed that the speed of a train might cause brain damage to passengers. Two centuries down the road, we're climbing onto roller-coasters and blasting into space with equanimity. And the best trains travel at around a hundred and eighty miles per hour. We value speed for the rush we get out of it. We also value speed because "time is money," and we want all the money and all the time we can get. Following this line of thought, the pleasure we get from speed is just another form of greed. And the nature of greed is that it cannot be satisfied by mere pleasure, no matter how great that pleasure is. I have read that greed is the opposite of contentment, and that makes sense. When I am contented, there is nothing I need and nothing I desire. When I feel greed, it is accompanied by frustration, experienced as a lack that can't be fulfilled. To quote Dudley Moore in the movie *Arthur*, I don't want enough; I want more than enough!

When we focus on the idea that time is money, we are tapping into a limitless greed because time is limitless, but our capacities are finite. I think it is healthier to decide that time is time, and money is money. And people are people. People need a certain amount of contentment in order to be creative, to be loving. Depriving ourselves of contentment precipitates a perversion of sorts as our human need for happiness twists itself into a desire for pleasure. Either we confuse pleasure with happiness, or we settle for what we can buy when we can't get what we really need. Either way, it results in misery and greed.

Happiness vs. Pleasure

The difference between happiness and pleasure is that pleasure is short-lived and requires greater and greater stimulants to remain pleasurable. I think of pleasure as existing on a continuum, so that a fifty-cent candy bar is a small pleasure and a fifty-thousand dollar Porsche Boxster is a greater pleasure. Because greed by its nature can't be satisfied, we tend to try greater and greater pleasures with the mistaken belief that eventually we will find a pleasure so great that we will feel contented. Happiness is binary: No one is ever a little happy – you're either happy or you're not.

I found myself writing about contentment and happiness as though they were the same thing, and I wondered if that might cause disagreements or confusion for you, my reader. So I want to explain my thoughts more fully.

In our culture, it seems like "happiness" has a stronger emotional loading than "contentment." Contentment is for the aged or for animals and babies. It is unthinking, even placid. Happiness, on the other hand, is what we reserve for people who fall in love or win the lottery. I think we confuse happiness with pleasure in these cases. Contentment implies a lack of excitement and innovation: Happiness is understood to be a temporary, but wonderful high. We underestimate contentment and overestimate happiness, and those two mistakes cause us to be unhappy, not because of what we're feeling when we're contented or happy, but because of the way we think about what we're feeling: The value we place on contentment as a concept is lower than the value we place on happiness. Isn't that strange?

Coming from a more Eastern viewpoint, contentment is the finest feeling we can aspire to, and is the essence of happiness, so I am using "contentment" and "happiness" interchangeably here.

Comfort

You don't hear people talking about comfort much, unless they're talking about a lack thereof. "I'm uncomfortable with . . ." is one statement we may hear in the workplace, and it's nearly often accompanied by feelings of hostility and anxiety because it's a politically correct way of saying, "I dislike this because . . ."

People rarely expect to comfort one another at work unless there is an extreme situation such as a death or accident that occurs during the workday. I even wonder if we believe that comfort is reserved for children or for those in immediate emotional distress. As much as I dislike the fatal effects of smoking, we once comforted each other by sharing a cigarette. There was something caring in being able to offer a colleague a smoke, removing the package from a pocket or purse, supplying a light, puffing together in companionable silence. Surely smoking was a comfort not only because of the rush of tar, nicotine, and other carcinogens into the unsuspecting lungs, but because it was portable and quick. The physical ritual was calming, and gave us something to do with our hands and mouths. The psychology of engaging the most sensitive parts of our bodies in a non-sexual manner allowed people to bond in direct but non-threatening ways. I think there was a lot to smoking as a social phenomenon that we have yet to explore.

We do bring coffee to each other when a meeting has gone badly or a proposal has failed, and although it gives the same message of caring, it's just not as immediate and portable as smoking. I suspect that the person who invents a way to produce two cups of scalding-hot coffee direct from a vest pocket will garner the appreciation of a significant percentage of the work force.

We have "comfort foods," which we indulge in when we hunger for more than food. Warm, heavy, usually caloric, reminding us of the days when food was prepared by family hands for our nourishment, not microwaved for speed. There is something soothing about mashed potatoes or oven-fresh cookies that can make the most self-reliant soul feel cared for, if only for a little while. Bringing comfort food into the workplace is a simple way to nurture people, especially as fewer and fewer people learn to cook food from scratch.

One burgeoning and very successful avenue of business these days is that of the nail shop. It's not a hardware store, it's a place where women can go for a manicure or pedicure. I was in Irvine, California, recently, and the nail shops outnumbered the coffeehouses at least three to one! How strange, I thought: I mean, they don't even cut hair in these places! How in the world could so many people be having their nails done!

Later, when I was reading *The Art of Happiness*, by the Dalai Lama and Howard C. Cutler, my bewilderment turned to awareness. Discussing Desmond Morris' book, *Intimate Behavior*, Cutler mentioned that we seek intimacy wherever we can find it, not just in what we recognize as intimate relationships. Among other things, he mentioned manicures as a way of being physically touched in a socially-acceptable way. Suddenly it made sense to me! Sure, having your nails done is a luxury: After all, with an emory board, some clippers and (for some) a bottle of ninety-nine cent polish, anyone can do a home manicure. But if the point is to [unconsciously] fulfill your need for the comfort of human contact, nail shops make complete sense. When was the last time someone held you hand for twenty minutes? The last time someone bathed and lotioned your feet? It is a comfort to be touched, even by a stranger, which also explains the popularity of massage therapy in a world where people who work together rarely even shake hands.

Physical as well as emotional comforts are important in the workplace. To work well, people need to have chairs, desks, and equipment that fit their bodies correctly. They need to move around enough so their joints don't get stiff, too. They need fresh air, reasonable room temperatures, access to food and water, and clean, safe spaces. Their phones and computers should work properly, or their drills and table saws, or their convection ovens and refrigerators. Ergonomics may not be a fashionable topic anymore, but it is still vital to the functioning of your employees (and you, too). You can help provide for the physical comfort of yourself and others by helping to keep workspaces clean. You can provide for the emotional comfort of others by being there for them when times get rough, and by using empathy, honesty, gentle humor, and good manners to keep the workplace emotionally clean.

Empowerment vs. Blame

As I mentioned earlier, in many cases of emergency or stress, the first thing people tend to do is look for someone to blame. I wonder if blaming is a habit we get into as children, when our parents make it clear that they don't care how the dog ended up covered head to toe with peanut butter, but want confessions from those who did it, Right Now! Parents have a good reason for preferring confessions because their job is to teach children to face up to the consequences of their actions and to tell the truth. In this case, a discussion of who did it is more important to the overall mission of the family. Besides, after the first few such incidents, parents understand that children will peanut butter the dog simply because they can (and because it seemed like a good idea at the time).

Criticism – Can You Take It?

"The surest way to make a monkey out of a man is to quote him."
- Robert Benchley

Throughout this book, I return to the idea that you stand or fall by the way you choose to communicate. Good leaders have to be able to express their ideas to other people. Good leaders also have to be able to listen, and not just to good news. Shooting the messenger is a long-established way of expressing one's dismay at the message, but the best leaders pay even more attention to the bad news. They want to know what mistakes they've made because they're more invested in solving the company's problems than they are in always looking good, personally. (These leaders also tend to arise in organizations where it's accepted that people make mistakes.) If you can't take criticism, if heads roll when you hear bad news, then your people can't trust you to make the best decisions when there's trouble afoot. Bad things will still happen, only you'll be the last to know.

Don't Niggle

Don't be cheap; it's contrary to the abundance thinking that is the essence of success. When you read books on how to be successful in business, folks like Deepak Chopra and Stephen Covey and Robert Kiyosaki agree that you have to think big, think generous. Nobody ever shrank to greatness! If you pay peanuts, you're gonna get monkeys. And even fine, intelligent people, if they aren't paid properly, will depreciate in value. Eventually, they will either become demoralized to the point of being worthless to the company or they'll go where they're recognized as valuable.

I knew a CEO who had his assistant drive all over town for a solid week talking to motel managers to try and "get a good deal" on motel rooms for managers who came in once a month for a meeting. He picked the cheapest motels and then tried to get them to reduce their prices a little more. The upshot of it was, he paid his assistant about $400 to get a $20 price reduction on motel rooms so crummy that his managers decided not to stay in them anyway. And his assistant quit out of raging boredom and the sense that she was wasting her life running errands for a fool.

**"I've worked myself up from nothing
to a state of supreme poverty."
- Groucho Marx**

"Nothing will work, unless
you do."
- John Wooden

Chapter Seven
Synergistic Leadership
- for Upper Management

Synergistic leadership zeroes in on the necessity for integrating the business, building integrity into the system, and empowering people to work. The Synergistic leader is most interested in acting in an ethical manner, building outstanding teamwork, placing respect for the individual in the center of work life, and creating outrageous customer service. The goal of the Synergistic leader is the Triple Win – processes whereby the company, the employees, the customers, all win. Triple Win isn't a catch-phrase; it's the daily expression of a set of core values that emphasizes cooperation, communication, and trust between employees, management, and customers. When you believe that people are the most important reason behind doing business, you naturally start to see that people are your major asset. When people at all levels of the organization feel valued, they respond with commitment, energy, and enthusiasm. These are the by-products of the Synergistic leader's search for establishing a firm, fair, and fun environment.

Bringing Synergy to your business is a proactive and continuous process of improvement based on building a culture of integrity in your organization. Rather than focusing on systems, it's time to take a good look at the people around you and at the level of trust that exists between management and employees. When you work on building trust, you are doing more than strengthening the interpersonal relationships so valuable to the healthy workplace: You are also setting standards that will determine the day-to-day and long-range success of your organization. When people work in a place where they can rely on each other and where they are needed, the feelings of belonging and emotional security motivate, energize, and inspire people to do their best work. When people are trusted, they are empowered to create new, highly effective ways of getting the job done. Letting people work at their best level is the first responsibility of management and the essence of bringing Synergy into the workplace.

> **"Management is doing things right;
> leadership is doing the right thing."
> - Peter F. Drucker**

Synergistic Team Leadership - for Middle Management

Synergistic team leadership encompasses the supervisors, middle managers, and department heads of the organization. Synergistic team leaders are the major catalysts for change in the organization, as they have the opportunity to coach, counsel, and mentor people through the changes instituted by extending the company focus to Synergy. If your team leaders aren't behind you on something as basic as reorienting your company values to focus on people, they will not be able to create the necessary changes for Synergistic success. On the other hand, if your team leaders are mature, sensitive people to whom communication and respect are already core values, you will have an easy time implementing new changes. Team leaders are in a position to apply the practical aspects of Synergy, and it's important that they know the importance of their place in the organizational scheme. Team leaders are in many ways the first to implement, motivate, recognize change or notice obstacles, and take further steps.

Successful team leaders lead by example, teaching and serving others while building an atmosphere of trust and empowerment. Synergistic team leaders work from a spiritual sense, valuing the idea that part of their job is to help others achieve. Synergistic team leadership requires a certain amount of confidence, as you need to be comfortable empowering your employees and trusting that they will do the right thing.

> ## "They say you have to use your best player first, but I found, you win with the ones that fit best together."
> ## - Vind Lombardi

Belief in Teamwork

Synergistic team leaders should start out with a commitment to teamwork and a belief that teamwork really is better than top-down decision-making. When team leaders are truly committed to teamwork, it shows, with the result that people actively want to work with them. Synergistic team leaders are charismatic, precisely because of their attitudes and values. People want to be needed; they want to participate, and it's a joy to work for someone who allows you to be your best.

The secret to building a great team involves rewarding team performance. Don't fall back into the old habit of picking out one hero: The hero is the team. Individuals can and should be rewarded for individual achievements but, in general, company goals require teamwork, and teams deserve recognition when they succeed.

Professionalism

Professionalism is paramount: People need to know that you are a straight-shooter, someone on whom they can rely. Being on time, keeping your word, making decisions in a reasonable and timely manner, these are all ways of expressing your professionalism. The way you use discipline also expresses your professional manner. Degrading people engenders resentment and fear, creating new problems without solving the old ones. Remember not to criticize the person but the behavior, and make sure to teach people correct behaviors rather than just telling them they're doing something wrong: Help them find ways to do it right.

The Joy of Goalsetting

All the willing team players in the world are no good to you until you have a set of solid goals. When everyone contributes to the goal-setting process, everyone has a reason to buy in, to be excited. Also, your employees will tend to set higher goals than you would expect, and joyfully achieve them, too!

"The human race has one really effective weapon, and that's laughter."
- Mark Twain

Kaizen: Continuous Improvement
"Kaizen" is the Japanese principle of improving little things every day. Use "baby steps" to create big changes a little bit at a time. Always seeking Synergy is one way to continuous improvement. Once your entire team is seeking Synergy in every part of your business, your organization will reinvent itself within a year, growing in prosperity and positive interactions.

Positive, Upbeat Leadership

"Laughter is the shortest distance between two people."
- Victor Borge

An enthusiastic leader is a wonderful asset to any organization. People like to work for positive, high-energy leaders because it makes them feel good. And when an organization is reinventing itself with Synergy as the goal, upbeat leadership is especially helpful. When companies are learning about teamwork, there is usually a honeymoon phase where it's easy to be upbeat. But the honeymoon is invariably followed by the realization that even Synergy takes work, commitment, and energy. Excellent leadership helps guide people through the day-to-day work of creating a new workplace.

In the third phase, it's easy for people to feel more

positive because the new internal changes are starting to show effects in better bottom lines and happier customers. The fourth phase is what everyone's looking for as people start to feel good about work, to want to instigate improvements, to be self-managed and motivated. By this time, upbeat leadership has taught other folks the great feelings that come with Synergy. Expect it to take at least a year before phase four makes an appearance, but enjoy the journey. It's such an exciting time, re-creating business as we've always known it! Take pleasure in the little, daily changes as well as the grand achievements that come along every few months.

Avoid Analysis Paralysis

Thinking too much can be as bad as not thinking at all, and overanalyzing is a fine way to put off having to do anything. I knew a man who got himself into graduate school because he didn't know what to do with his life and then couldn't decide what to specialize in. He was miserable in his department and checked out several others, but he just couldn't make a choice. He thought about it and talked about it with everyone he knew, everyone he met, until he had no friends left. He had a girlfriend, but she left him after a couple of years, only being able to take so much discussion about his indecision. He was truly stuck until his department told him it was time to put out or get out. He had no more choices, no more time to dilly-dally. And he rose to the occasion just fine. He dashed off a dissertation in no time and ran out the door with a Ph.D. tucked under his arm.

People who are stuck in analysis paralysis are either having a good time thinking and don't really care if they produce something, or are tortured by indecision and hope that if they just think long and hard enough, a solution will eventually present itself. If you find yourself suffering from analysis paralysis, turn to others for help, or even delegate the problem. I once read somewhere that, if you are really stuck between two choices, you should get a quarter and flip it. If it lands on heads and you feel disappointed, choose tails (after all, it's your decision and your quarter, too). If you really can't decide, let the coin choose for you.

Sometimes people get stuck because they don't have all the information they need. Say it's your task to choose between two health-care plans for the company and you just can't decide. One has lower premiums, but one has lower co-pays. One has great dental coverage, one has excellent vision coverage. Neither one has everything, of course. Your deadline is getting close! What can you do?

You might consider referring the problem to the company employees. Present the two packages, and take a vote. Not only have you made your decision based on what the majority of people prefer, you have also acted inclusively, letting people know that their input is valued. Problem solved.

Motivate, Communicate

Humor is a helpful way to make work fun, and doesn't detract from the idea that you also expect the best from your people. Start by trusting that employees can do a great job and make sure to give them the training they need to meet and exceed your expectations. Teaching, coaching, and counseling help employees become successful, and when done correctly, build your relationship with them as well. A large part of your job involves listening to and talking with people, finding out what inspires them, what turns them on, and finding ways to bring excitement into the workplace in the service of your stated goals. Management By Wandering Around (MBWA) is a great way to get to know what makes your people tick and what makes them succeed.

Growing a great business is more than having great relationships: You also have to have a great product. Great relationships can create a great and ever-improving product as team members band together to increase quality of workmanship, to bring new ideas to the table. Part of your responsibility is to accept nothing less than total quality and to inspire the rest of your team to feel the same way. Using FAD (Fanatical Attention to Detail), cross-training and continued education, teams are always adjusting the way they work and thinking about ways to make the products and services better.

So, What's Your Gig?

"Learn to play from the same sheet of music."

If you think of your organization as a musical group, what kind would it be? A tremendous orchestra with hundreds of strings, winds, and a full percussion section? Or a quiet little trio that plays on the street corner? Maybe you're part of a cool jazz ensemble, dark glasses even indoors, suits and silk ties, and fedoras and shiny shoes. Or is your gig something a little rougher, a little younger, something body-pierced, bright-haired, and loud?

This is a game to help you think creatively about the kind of company you keep. Like a group of musicians, a company is a living, breathing organism that, under ideal circumstances, works together. Some groups have a formally designated conductor. In others, people agree on a beat and start together. Groups that practice together in smaller groups and then meet for an all-orchestra rehearsal have the chance to work out musical problems in shorter periods of time. Groups that don't bother to tune up together tend to make a mess. Take a minute to think about your organization as though it's a group of musicians, then you might want to play with ideas of how to make your music (your products, systems, and services) more . . . harmonious. Is your product wonderful? Does it satisfy the customer? Is it delivered on time? When customers have problems, are the issues resolved with goodwill and grace? Does everyone know the score? This is the sound of a Symphony of Excellence!

Commit to People and Service

Committing to people can be the most rewarding experience in your work life. However, there are some people who don't especially value other people or even want to work with them! Some people are afraid of others, in which case it becomes really difficult to commit to spending more time with them, listening to their needs, and providing answers for them. There may be some leaders who shouldn't be around people at all! Smart but asocial leaders hire other people (preferably people who don't need much supervision or feedback) to deflect some of the social obligations that come with the job. If, in general, you like people and don't find them frightening, committing to their well-being is an easy thing to do. Committing to service is also easy if it's attached to the idea that service means helping people. Service, when you take it out of the context of people, becomes nebulous.

Synergistic leadership requires the willingness to help people: other managers, employees and customers, the community. When you commit to people

and service, you are building something bigger than a network, you are building a way of life for your organization.

Commit to Quality Products

The business world is a pretty tricky place: Not many years ago, a woman would buy a bathing suit for summer vacation. Now, most women's bathing suit pieces are sold separately – with each piece costing what an entire suit once did. Soon, we'll be buying individual socks! The folks who make yogurt and potato chips figured out that rather than raising prices all the time, they could make their products just a bit smaller, and that people would pay the same price they'd always been paying. Supermarkets invented a card system, so if you don't have a card for that market, you pay 50% more or even sometimes twice as much because their "sale" prices only apply to people who have the card. And there are very few real sales, because now *everything* is "on sale."

All these little insults to the consumer add up – people aren't stupid. We notice when our eight-ounce yogurt becomes a six-ounce yogurt, and it ticks us off. We also notice when things wear out fast or don't do what they should do in the first place.

When you think about product quality, it's incumbent upon you to think about the customer who will be pleased or disappointed. Excellent workmanship, fine materials, well-thought out delivery systems, and outrageously good customer service are imperative in a culture of integrity. You shouldn't feel embarrassed or nervous about the products you sell, and when a company sells a good product, sales are bolstered by customers who are also employees. When an organization's employees don't want to purchase the product, there is something wrong, either with the product or with the organization that has failed its workers so completely that they are unwilling to contribute to its coffers.

Beyond the Bottom Line

> "Happiness... it lies in the joy of
> achievement, in the thrill of
> creative effort."
> - Franklin D. Roosevelt

Once you decide to embrace Synergy in your organization, an old notion may intrude upon you, causing you to waver. Known as "the bottom line," it has been cherished by business leaders for centuries. It's probably been the first love of many executives! But the bottom line is a cruel mistress. She can cause people to make short-term deals at a long-term cost, as when oil companies destroy wildlife habitat in pursuit of higher profits. Layoffs are all about the bottom line, as are the decisions that reduce the quality of life of the employees, the quality of the prod-

uct, the satisfaction of the customer. In fact, you really do have to spend money to make money, and being cheap about the needs of your people results in frequent hiring, retraining, and absenteeism. Being cheap tells your workers (and customers, too) what the real values are in the organization, and it decreases their trust and respect.

Of course, a company has to make a profit! But there should be some consideration of how big the profit needs to be in order to be successful, and how much money can be channeled into long-term profits — things that increase the stability of the employee base, that improve the product, that keep the customers happy and loyal.

In a book published in the '70s called *Ecotopia*, the author, Ernest Callenbach, posed the idea of financial cost versus social cost and built a Utopic vision around the balance between the two. The most radical change was the abolition of gas-powered machines, so that the [few] automobiles and trains ran on electricity. Without cars, streets were narrowed to bike lanes, providing easier access for people who wanted to run, walk, skate, or bicycle to work. Increased exercise and greatly improved air quality improved the health of the general public; a good thing, since society provided free health care to everyone. What made the book appealing to some people and threatening to others was the idea that the simple, determined implementation of core values could cause such drastic social change. I think we like to believe that some changes are too difficult to approach: this book pointed out that it's a matter of will and of being brave enough to say, "This is what I believe in, so this is what I'll do."

A number of companies exist exclusively for the bottom line, and they will not be able to make the leap to Synergy. In the end, though, companies that implement Synergy will be the ones that survive in the competitive business world.

Can you tell how much money is lost when employees are unhappy and unsupported in their work? Probably not. But in companies that have been willing to make the leap from the bottom line to concentrating on their core values, the profits are realized in figures that exceed those of companies where the bottom line reigns supreme. If senior managers believe that Synergy is a good strategy, that belief provides the support for the rest of the organization. If senior management just pays lip-service to ideas such as respect and empowerment of employees, that lack of belief will be obvious when policy does not reflect important values necessary for building Synergy. It's as simple as that.

Some people aren't cut out for being leaders because they value personal power over the creation of Synergy. They can't let go of their fears long enough to replace insecurity and mistrust with optimism and teamwork. But most people can certainly achieve Synergistic leadership as long as they feel assured that upper-level management supports their endeavors.

Silence and Creativity

**"True silence is the rest of the mind;
it is to the spirit what sleep is
to the body, nourishment and
refreshment"
- William Penn**

I want to briefly discuss the contribution of silence in productive work. Silence is something people both want and fear. I want the kids next door to be quiet so I can think, but thinking in a silent house reminds me that I'm totally alone and cast upon my own fragile resources. Some people can't bear to be alone. I knew a woman once who had come from a family split by selfishness and insanity. Her memories must have been agonizing and constant: She simply couldn't be alone with them. She would hire extra staff to man her office – not to free her up to work, but to keep her company. Her employees were chronically confused, being given a job description that didn't include the majority of their work, which was babysitting the boss. The fact that she was querulous and bad-tempered only made things worse, as she expected employees to drop whatever they were doing whenever she wanted to have a conversation about sex, religion, or politics. (I think she chose those inappropriate topics because in her family, it was not alright to have privacy or personal boundaries, and she was recreating in her office what she had experienced in childhood.) It drove her employees crazy, working for someone who not only violated their privacy of beliefs, but who wouldn't let them alone to do their work.

People who have too much silence can go crazy, hearing voices, becoming obsessive. There is a legitimate reason to fear too much silence, but silence is like water; you can drown in it or die from its lack. Creativity needs a certain amount of brooding, of quiet and reflection. Businesspeople make the mistake of thinking that they should always look busy, and believe that silence is reserved for hermits and artists. If you want to bring artistry to your work, try practicing at least ten or twenty minutes of silence every day, and watch your creativity increase. Also, realize that other people need silence in order to muse, to imagine, and to create. When someone takes on a new project, encourage that person to spend some time alone reflecting on their new challenge.

A Note of Encouragement

If you're feeling overwhelmed, remember that you don't have to be perfect in order to achieve Synergy and all its benefits. Mostly, you have to want to try! Joyful leadership is about knowing where you stand and communicating your stance to others in such a way that they are excited about joining your quest. If you know what matters to you, can set reasonable and challenging goals, hire people of integrity, involve everyone in marketing and celebrating successes, you are creating an excellent environment for Synergy.

If you do these things and apply the strategies that we've talked about . . . I will see you on the crest of a joyful wave!

"No amount of money,
or material value can
replace the feeling of
being totally, and
completely saturated
with love, laughter and
joy, and you get it by
giving it away."

Selected Bibliography

Albion, Mark. *Making a Life, Making a Living.* New York: Warner Books, 2000.

Albrecht, Carl. *At America's Service.* New York: Warner Books, Inc., 1992.

Alexander, Chris. *Creating Extraordinary Joy*, San Jose, CA: Hunter House, 2001.

Allen, James. *As a Man Thinketh*, Mount Vernon, NY: The Peter Pauper Press, date not listed.

American Bible Society. *The Good News Bible.* Glasgow, Great Britain: William Collins Sons and Company Limited, 1976.

Autry, James. *Real Power.* New York: Riverhead Books, 1998.

Barker, Joel Arthur. *Paradigms: The Business of Discovering the Future.* New York: HarperCollins Publishers Inc., 1992.

Beatty, Jack. *The World According to Peter Drucker.* New York: The Free Press, 1998.

Bennis, Warren. *On Becoming a Leader.* Reading, MA: Addison-Wesley Publishing Company, 1989.

Berne, Eric. *Games People Play.* New York: Grove Press, 1964.

Blanchard, Kenneth and Spencer Johnson. *The One Minute Manager.* New York: Berkley Books, 1982.

Borysenko, Joan and Miroslav. *The Power of the Mind to Heal.* Carlsbad, CA: Hay House, 1996.

Buscaglia, Leo F. *Living, Loving & Learning.* New York: Ballantine Books, 1983.

Butler, Gillian and Tony Hope. *Managing Your Mind.* New York: Oxford University Press, 1995.

Byham, William C. *Zapp! The Lighting of Empowerment.* New York: Ballantine Books, 1988.

Capodagli, Bill & Lynn Jackson. *The Disney Way.* New York: McGraw-Hill, 1999.

Castaneda, Carlos. *The Teaching of Don Juan ... a Yaqui Way of Knowledge.* New York: Pocket Books, 1977.

Chang, Richard. *The Passion Plan at Work.* San Francisco, CA: Jossey-Bass Publishers, 2001.

Chopra, Deepak. *Unconditional Life.* New York: Bantam Books, 1992.

______. *Return of the Rishi.* Boston, MA: Houghton Mifflin Company, 1991.

______. *To Know God.* New York: Harmony Books, 2000.

Collins, Jim. *Good to Great.* New York: HarperCollins Publishers Inc., 2001.

Covey, Stephen R. *Principle-Centered Leadership.* New York: Simon & Schuster, 1992.

Csikszentmihalyi, Mihaly. *Flow.* New York: Harper and Row, Publishers, Inc., 1990.

Davidson: Learning Org. Organizational Behavior 9th Edition, Herrigel, Slocum, Woodman 2001, Pg 522-523

Davis, Phyllis K. *The Power of Touch.* Carlsbad, CA: Hay House, Inc., 1991.

Dell, Chip R. *Managers as Mentors.* San Francisco, CA: Berrett-Koehler Publishers, Inc., 1996.

Dotlich, David L. and Peter C. Cairo. *Action Coaching.* San Francisco, CA: Jossey-Bass Publishers, 1999.

Drucker, Peter F. *The New Realities.* New York: Harper and Row Publishers, 1989.

______. *Management Challenges for the Twenty First Century.* New York: HarperCollins Publishers Inc., 1999.

Dyer, Wayne W. *Wisdom of the Ages.* New York: HarperCollins Publishers Inc., 1998.

Elkin, Allen. *Stress Management for Dummies.* Foster City, CA: IDG Books Worldwide, Inc., 1999.

Exley, Helen. *In Praise and Celebration of Love,* New York: Exley Publications Ltd., 1995.

Foundation for Inner Peace. *A Course in Miracles.* Huntington Station, NY: Foundation for Inner Peace, 1979.

Freiberg, Kevin and Jackie. *Nuts! Southwest Airlines' Crazy Recipe for Business and Personal Success.* Austin, TX: Bard Press, 1996.

Fuller, R. Buckminster. *Synergetics-Explorations in the Geometry of Thinking.* New York: MacMillan Publishers, 1975.

Gallo, Fred P. *Energy Psychology.* Boca Raton, FL: CRC Press, 1999.

Gerber, Michael. *The E-Myth Manager.* New York: HarperCollins Publishers Inc., 1998.

Gittell, Jody Hoffer. *The Southwest Airlines' Way.* New York: McGraw-Hill, 2003.

Goleman, Daniel. *Emotional Intelligence.* New York: Bantam Books, 1995.

Greenleaf, Robert K. *On Becoming a Servant Leader.* Edited by Frick, Don M. & Spears, Larry C. San Francisco, CA: Jossey-Bass Publishers, 1996.

Hanh, Thich Nhat. *Living Budda, Living Christ.* New York: Riverhead Books, 1995.

Harris, Judith Parker. *Conquer Crisis with Health-esteem.* Beverly Hills, CA: Saywrite Publications, 1998.

Harvey, Andrew. *Teachings of Rumi,* Boston, MA: Shambhala Books, 1999.

Hay, Louise L. *Heal Your Body.* Carlsbad, CA: Hay House, Inc., 1988.

Henricks, Mark. *Grow Your Business.* Irvine, CA: Entrepreneur Press, 2001.

Hill, Napoleon. *Think and Grow Rich.* North Hollywood, CA: Wilshire Book Company, 1966.

______. *Law of Success.* Chicago, IL: Success Unlimited, Inc., 1979.

Hillman, James. *The Soul's Code.* New York, Random House, 1996.

Hogan, Eve Eschner with Steven. *Intellectual Foreplay.* Alameda, CA: Hunter House, 2000.

Holmes, Ernest. *The Science of Mind*. New York: Dodd, Mead and Company, 1938.

Jampolsky, Gerald. *Love is Letting Go of Fear*. Berkeley, CA: Celestial Arts, 1979.

John Paul II, His Holiness. *Crossing the Threshold of Hope*. New York: Random House, 1994.

Keen, Sam. *To Love and Be Loved*. New York: Bantam Books, 1997.

Kouzes, James M. and Barry Z. Posner. *The Leadership Challenge*. San Francisco, CA: Jossey-Bass Publishers, 1995.

Kuhn, Robert Lawrence. *Closer to Truth*. New York: McGraw-Hill, 2000.

Lager, Fred "Chico". *Ben & Jerry's: The Inside Scoop*, New York: Crown Publishing Group; Reprint edition (June 1995).

Lama, The Dalai. *The Joy of Living and Dying in Peace*. New York: HarperCollins Publishers Inc., 1991.

______. *The Art of Happiness*. New York: Riverhead Books, 1998.

Leadership . . . with a Human Touch. Jan 18, 1994, May 10, 1994, May 9, 1995, June 6, 1995. Economics Press, Inc., Fairfield, New Jersey.

Lindbergh, Anne Morrow. *Gifts from the Sea*. New York: Pantheon Book, Inc., 1955.

Maltz, Maxwell. *Psycho-Cybernetics*. Hollywood, CA: Wilshire Book Company, 1965.

Mandino, Og. *The Greatest Salesman in the World*. New York: Bantam Books, 1968.

______. *The Greatest Miracle in the World*. New York: Bantam Books, 1975.

______. *The Greatest Salesman in the World, Part II*, New York: Bantam Books, 1988.

Mann, Nancy R. *The Keys to Excellence. The Deming Philosophy*. London, England: Mercury Books, 1989.

McBryde, Linda. *The Mass Market Woman*. Eagle River, AK: Crowded Hour Press, 1999.

McWilliams, John-Roger & Peter. *Life 101: You Can't Afford the Luxury of a Negative Thought*. Los Angeles, CA: Prelude Press, 1988.

______. *Life 101*. Los Angeles, CA: Prelude Press, 1991.

Montrose, Philip. *Getting through to Your Emotions with EFT.* Sacramento, CA: Holistic Communications, 2000.

Moore, Thomas. *Original Self*. New York: HarperCollins Publishers Inc., 1981.

Nerburn, Kent and Louise Mengelkoch. *Native American Wisdom*. San Rafael, CA: New World Library, 1991.

Nerburn, Kent. *The Soul of an Indian*. San Rafael, CA: New World Library, 1993.

Noel, Brooke. *Back to Basics*. Beverly Hills, CA: Champion Press, 1999.

Novak, Philip. *The World's Wisdom*. Edison, NJ: Castle Books, 1996.

Ornish, Dean. *Love and Survival: The Scientific Basis for the Healing Power of Intimacy*. New York: HarperCollins Publishers Inc., 1998.

Palmer, Parker J. *Active Life*. San Francisco, CA: Jossey-Bass Publishers, 1990.

______. *Let your Life Speak*. San Francisco, CA: Jossey-Bass Publishers, 2000.

Pearsall, Paul. *The Pleasure Prescription*. Alameda, CA: Hunter House, 1998.

Peck, M. Scott. *The Road Less Traveled*. New York: Simon & Schuster, 1978.

Pert, Candace and Deepak Chopra. *Molecules of Emotion*. New York: Scribner, 1997.

Peters, Thomas J. and Robert H. Waterman, Jr. *In Seach of Excellence*. New York: Warner Books, 1982.

______. *Thriving on Chaos*. New York: Harper Perennial, 1987.

______. *Liberation Management*. New York: Alfred A. Knopf, 1992.

Powell, John. *Unconditional Love*. Allen, TX: Argus Communications, 1978.

Redfield, James. *The Celestine Prophecy*. New York: Warner Books, 1993.

Richards, Dick. *Artful Work*. San Francisco, CA: Berrett-Koehler Publishers, Inc., 1995.

Robbins, Anthony. *Awaken the Giant Within*. New York: Summit Books, 1991.

Russell, Peter. *The Brain Book*. New York: Penguin Group, 1979.

Simon, David. *Vital Energy*. New York: Wiley, 2000.

Spector, Robert and Patrick D. McCarthy. *The Nordstrom's Way: The Inside Story of America's # 1 Customer Service Company*. New York: John Wiley and Sons, Inc., 1995.

Stanley, Andy. *Visioneering*. Sisters, OR: Multnomah Publishers, Inc., 1999.

Star, Jonathan. *Rumi*. New York: Penguin Putnam, Inc., 1997.

Steward, Marjabelle Young and Marian Faux. *Executive Etiquette in the New Workplace*. New York: St. Martin's Press, 1994.

Thomas, R. David. *Dave's Way*. New York: Berkley Books, 1992.

Thoreau, Henry David. *Walden and Other Writings*. New York: Barnes & Noble Books, 1993.

Tracy, Brian. *The 100 Absolutely Unbreakable Laws of Business Success*. San Francisco, CA: Berrett-Koehler Publishers, Inc., 2000.

______. *Advance Selling Strategies*. New York: Simon & Schuster, 1995.

Trimble, Vance H. *Sam Walton, Founder of Walmart*. New York: Penguin Books, 1990.

Weil, Andrew. *Spontaneous Healing*. New York: Ballentine Books, 1996.

Welch, Jack. *Jack, Straight from the Gut.* New York: Warner Books, Inc., 2001.

Wheatley, Margaret J. and Myron Kellner-Rogers, *A Simpler Way.* San Francisco, CA: Berrett-Koehler, 1996.

Wolf, Fred Alan. *Mind into Matter.* Portsmouth, NH: Moment Point Press, 2001.

Young, Willa A. *Happiness Instruction Kit.* Santa Barbara, CA: The Williams Groups, 2002.

Ziff, Lazer. *Ralph Waldo Emerson - Selected Essays.* New York: Penguin Books, 1984.

Zingheim, Patricia K. and J.R. Schuster. *Pay People Right.* San Francisco, CA: Jossey-Bass Publishers, 2000.

Zukav, Gary. *The Seat of the Soul.* New York: Fireside, 1989.

Synergizing Your Business
A Train-the-Trainer Business Building System

Synergizing Your Business is a cost effective, on-site, train-the-trainer program. Synergizing Your Business teaches you to coach your team to greatness by showing you step-by-step how to build a high-performance team, satisfy customers, and deliver outstanding bottom line results.

This is the ultimate business building program for small business owners, branch managers, retail managers, and corporate department heads.

Synergizing Your Business includes:
- Synergizing Your Business Handbook
- Synergizing Your Business Audio Album with 6 Cassettes/CDs
- Synergizing Your Business Train-the-Trainer Workshop
- Synergizing Your Business Leader's Guide
- Synergizing Your Business Workbook Masters/disk
- Synergizing Your Business Video
- Synergizing Your Business Leader's Introduction CD/Tape
- Synergy Business Partners – a monthly round table business building meeting, business advisers – resource guide, and on-line advice. (Optional)

You will learn:
- Leadership skills that will focus your business towards success.
- How to motivate your employees through effective supervision.
- How to build a high—performance team.
- Tried and tested techniques for exceeding customer expectations.
- How to increase sales through Synergistic Sales Power.

Easy to implement:
This package includes a train-the-trainer workshop and a complete systems' guide for easy and simple implementation. All it takes is a short 1° hour meeting every week for 10 weeks and your team will begin to achieve the extraordinary. Total package only = **$499.00 USA**

In addition, it is vital to attend the Synergy Business Partners round table meetings once a month.

Orders:
Tel. 949/586-0511   esynergy@pacbell.net
www.SynergyLifeMastery.com

Speaking Presentations, Seminars, and Workshops

Chris Alexander's Synergy presentations are designed to assist businesses, associations, and organizations build dynamic, motivated, purpose-driven individuals, who understand the importance of working together, to achieve the extraordinary in their personal and business lives.

Business Topics:

Leadership
Synergistic Leadership * Synergistic Team Leadership

Team Building, Relationship Management
Synergistic Teamwork Boot Camp * Synergistic Team Building *
Synergy Behavior Matrix * Building Trust in the Workplace

Motivation and Attitudinal
Synergy Life Mastery * Got Joy? * Reaching Your Goals *
Strategies for Personal Power * RelaxAction Stress Management

Communication
Synergy Behavior Matrix * Effective Communication *
Effective Meetings * Humor in the Workplace

Sales Power
Synergistic Sales Power – 6 Steps to Effective Selling

Executive Coaching
CEO and Senior Executive One-to-One and Team Coaching

Custom Designed Training Programs and Presentations

For availability and rates:
Tel: 949/586-0511   esynergy@pacbell.net
www.SynergyLifeMastery.com

Creating Extraordinary Joy
by Chris Alexander

Extraordinary joy is freedom from the roller-coaster of daily highs and lows that most of us experience. It is a state of deep satisfaction and continuous delight that comes when we really like who we are, how we live with others, and what we do in life. The key to this is *Synergy*: making connections that energize and inspire us beyond the ordinary. It could be a connection with our own mental, emotional, and spiritual levels or with a loving partner, a respected colleague, or a community or group. Acting in *Synergy* brings us to a whole new level of happiness.

Using inspirational teachings from traditional and contemporary sources, images from nature, powerful exercises, and real-life examples from workshops and seminars, Chris Alexander describes the seven steps that can put *Synergy* into your life. Each step yields a life lesson that allows you to break free from patterns of behavior that cause guilt, hurt, and fear.

These lessons include:
* understanding *Synergy* and making it work for you
* recognizing *all* your available life choices
* clearing out old ideas that cause you pain
* making choices that express the needs of your true self
* living up to your higher purpose
* achieving your goals
* staying connected with the joy you've found

Creating Extraordinary Joy will inspire you to make choices that fulfill your deepest needs. You will learn to envision – and create – the most important sort of happiness: an immoderately, exuberantly joyful life.

- $15.95 USA

Orders:
Tel. 949/586-0511 esynergy@pacbell.net
www.SynergyLifeMastery.com

Synergy Life Mastery Audio Album
by Chris Alexander

Achieve Extraordinary Success and Joy in
Your Personal and Business Life

Six powerful Synergy audio cassettes that are all designed to motivate and
inspire you to have more rewarding relationships, improve your financial
status, and achieve happiness and joy.

Listen and learn these powerful Synergy Life Mastery strategies:

Tape 1: The Phenomenon of Synergy and Cleansing the Inner Self

Tape 2: Thought and Emotional Cleansing

Tape 3: Pro-Active Choices and Achieving a Sense of Purpose

Tape 4: The First Spiritual Expression . . . Love and Envisioning the
   Future

Tape 5: Setting and Reaching your Goals

Tape 6: RelaxAction and Focusing Mind Energy

-$69.00 USA

For Information and Orders:
Tel. 949/586-0511 esynergy@pacbell.net
www.SynergyLifeMastery.com

Synergizing Your Business
"5 Outrageous and Outstanding Bridges To Power Up Your Business"
by Chris Alexander

"Alexander debunks common leadership myths and discusses how Synergy prevents errors that cost companies and shareholders millions."
When the leadership of a company embraces the principle of Synergy . . . sales, customer service, net income, and cash flow grows.

Learning to Go Beyond the Bottom Line
Alexander's new book demonstrates the importance of leadership commitment to honest, direct communication for the good of the entire organization. *Synergizing Your Business* goes far beyond merely teaching "listening skills": It addresses the vital need for effective, respectful, mannerly communication at all levels of the company. Alexander debunks 15 common leadership myths and discusses preventable errors that cost companies millions and goes *beyond the need for greed.*

Triple Win Principle
The basis of this compelling book is the concept of "Synergy," by which the whole becomes greater than the sum of its parts: when Synergizing people connect in powerful, lasting, and ultra-effective ways. Destructive interpersonal competition is replaced by concerted, wholehearted effort. Synergy, which creates mutual trust, motivation, and concern throughout the organizational hierarchy, is *the new wave of business leadership.* Synergistic Leadership reinforces a passionate believe in a *Triple Win Principle.* Triple Win means choosing a broader perspective in how we conduct business on a daily basis. It focuses on the company winning, the employees winning, and the customer winning.

Creating Joy in the Workplace
In this groundbreaking business book, Alexander describes how to create excellence at every level of the organization. The techniques in *Synergizing Your Business*, previously only available to those who attend Synergy Executive Education seminars, elevates middle managers and salespeople, while also satisfying and educating seasoned business executives. Managers and staff can easily apply the concepts individually and become more effective and satisfied at work, or impact the wider organization by implementing enhanced training, clarifying communication, and creating a *camaraderie and joy rarely found in the ordinary workplace.*

$12.95 USA

Orders:
Tel. 949/586-0511 esynergy@pacbell.net
www.SynergyLifeMastery.com